Islam
Its Beauty & Wisdom

Dr. Gohar Mushtaq

amana publications

First Edition
(1431AH/2010AC)

© Copyright 1431AH/2010AC
amana publications
10710 Tucker Street
Beltsville, Maryland 20705-2223 USA
Tel: (301) 595-5999 / Fax: (301) 595-5888
E-mail: amana@igprinting.com
Website: www.amana-publications.com

Library of Congress Cataloging-in-Publication Data

Mushtaq, Gohar, 1971-
  Islam, its beauty and wisdom / Gohar Mushtaq. -- 1st ed.
     p. cm.
  ISBN 978-1-59008-060-3
  1. Islam. 2. Islam--Essence, genius, nature. I. Title.
  BP163.M932 2010
  297.2--dc22

                                    2010002497

PRINTED IN THE UNITED STATES OF AMERICA

International Graphics
10710 Tucker Street,
Beltsville, Maryland 20705-2223
Tel: (301) 595-5999
Fax: (301) 595-5888

Website: igprinting.com

Table of Contents

Foreword
by Jeffrey Bernstein

HAVING BEEN RAISED IN THE JEWISH faith, at a young age, I attended the obligatory Hebrew school. As a point of reference, Hebrew school is much the same as Sunday school is for those of the Christian faith. Always being an inquisitive person by nature, I asked the teacher that if Jesus Christ was not truly the son of God, as you have taught me, then why at the very least is he not recognized by Judaism as a Prophet for his great teachings. Again I questioned the teacher, why is not Muhammad (peace be upon him) seen as a Prophet by Jews for his great teachings? The Teacher at this point, probably never having been asked such questions before, or at least not in this form or venue, told me that they were considered just men but not Prophets. I replied that were not the Prophets Moses and Abraham just men as well? Were their teachings and actions any more important than Jesus or Muhammad (peace be upon him)? By this time he had enough and threw me out of the class, my questions basically unresolved.

That is why this book *Islam – Its Beauty and Wisdom* by Dr. Gohar Mushtaq is so important. It seeks to try and answer part of that question I had asked in Hebrew School, what are the great teachings of the Prophet Muhammad (peace be upon him) that was revealed to him by Allah.

This book first explains what the five pillars of Islam are in such a way any non-Muslim can understand and appreciate. It then heads in a direction I have never personally seen before in any religious manuscript. By this, I mean it provides us with effective scientific reasoning to explain health benefits associated with performing obligatory prayers (*salah*) and fasting (*saw'm*). As someone similar to Dr. Mushtaq with an extensive background in the Life Sciences, I can certainly appreciate this approach. He explains how the timing of the five prayers during the day can aid in maintaining good health. The prayers in the early morning, late afternoon, and after sunset are shorter because they are performed on an empty stomach. The noon and evening prayers are longer because these occur after meals. These longer prayers provide exercise for the person. Why exercise, you ask, it is because prayer in Islam involves standing, bowing and prostrations. The movements are mild, uniform and involve all muscles and joints. Calories are burned, blood-flow is increased to the brain, mental concentration is improved, and muscles below the lungs are compressed leading to better breathing. In addition, prostration leads to a drainage of sinus and hence prevents sinusitis, which is an affliction that I have had to suffer with for years. This is the original exercise program so to speak, that Allah in his wisdom provided us with 1,400 years ago.

Then we have revealed the health benefits of fasting (*Saw'm*). In laboratory animals, restricting caloric intake actually increased longevity and the reduced incidence of age-related disease. The fasting body burns toxins first and then stored nutrients. The immune system is also strengthened. As Dr. Mushtaq states, "Fasting gives your organs a rest and helps reverse the aging process for a longer and healthier life."

Even the very act of Wudu or the rinsing of face, hands, and feet with clean water before prayer has a medical benefit, to remove bacteria and viruses for example. This is exactly what we are being told right now by medical authorities to emphasize in the wake of the swine flu hysteria sweeping the World.

The health benefits of charity (*zakah*) are also explored in depth, something I think no non-Muslim would have even considered, and very timely at this juncture in time with the world economy in the state it is in.

According to Dr. Mushtaq, the five pillars are just the building blocks of Islam. In order to complete the building, one should also be observing the moral codes of Islam for being a good human being. One should also excel in optional faith-building acts as well. This emphasizes the fact that Islam is not just a religion but a way of life.

Congregational prayer teaches that collective benefits of the society are more important than individual benefits. This is how the Japanese structure their society and something we should really be thinking about in the West, since our individualistic approach has led to corruption, malaise and economic decline.

This collective attitude of Islam is also seen in the chapters concerning the pilgrimage (*Hajj*). Malcolm X on his *Hajj* had an epiphany (as had others). He states, "I saw that tens of thousands of pilgrims from all over the world of all colors could come together in one place, participate in the same ritual, and display a spirit of unity and brotherhood that my experiences in America had led me to believe never could exist between the white and non-white."

Malcolm X upon returning to the U.S. rejected the teachings of the Black Muslim movement, which preached race separation. He then announced his conversion to orthodox Islam and in the brotherhood of blacks and whites. He stressed that the spiritual lessons of his *Hajj* must be extended to non-Muslims as well as Muslims, blacks as well as whites. He was assassinated for attempting to do this by the Black Muslim movement.

This manuscript made such an impact on me as to inspire me to go back and reread the Autobiography of Malcolm X. As Malcolm said, "America needs to understand Islam, because this is the one religion that erases from its society the race problem."

If one really wants to understand Islam, then I can think of no better place to start than this book by Dr. Mushtaq.

Jeffrey Bernstein, (MS, Molecular Biology)
Devon, Pennsylvania

Introduction

THE WORD "ISLAM" HAS TWO-FOLD MEANINGS: submission to God (Allah)[1] and peace. This submission requires a fully conscious and willing effort to submit to the One Almighty God. This means to act on what Allah enjoins all of us to do (in the Qur'an) and what His beloved Prophet Muhammad (peace be upon him) encouraged us to do in his *sunnah* (his lifestyle and sayings personifying the Qur'an).

Once we submit totally to Allah, in faith and in action, we will surely feel peace and tranquility in our hearts. This, in turn, will bring about peace in our external conduct as well. Islam is careful to remind us that it is not merely a religion but a complete way of life that must be practiced continuously for it to be Islam. The Muslim must practice the five pillars of the religion: the declaration of faith in the oneness of Allah and the prophethood of Muhammad (peace be upon him), prayer, fasting the month of Ramadan, *zakah* (compulsory charity), and the pilgrimage to Makkah; and believe in the six articles of faith: belief in God, the Holy Books, the prophets, the angels, the Day of Judgment and God's decree, whether for good or ill.

There are other commandments of Islam, which encompass almost all aspects of one's personal, family, and civic life. These include such matters as diet, clothing, personal hygiene, interpersonal relations, business ethics, responsibilities towards parents, spouse and children, marriage, divorce and inheritance, civil and criminal law, etc.

---

[1] **A note to readers:** The Arabic word "Allah" is equivalent to "God" in English. However, linguistically, the word "Allah" is much more precise than "God" in its meanings. There is no gender, male or female, associated with the word "Allah" in Arabic, whereas the term "God" is masculine and its feminine is "goddess." Similarly, there is no plural for "Allah," whereas the plural for "God" is "gods." The word "Allah" is a proper name of God, through which man calls upon God personally. The name "Allah" is not confined to Islam; it is also the name by which Arabic-speaking Christians of the Oriental churches call upon God.

WHAT DO MUSLIMS BELIEVE?

Muslims believe in an unseen Ultimate Creator, source of all the physical and spiritual power that exists in the universe. The Islamic creed of Tawheed (unity of God) is summed up in the Qur'an as follows:

"Say: He is Allah, the One and Only.
Allah is He on Whom all depend.
He begets not, nor is He begotten.
And there is none comparable unto Him."
(Surah Al-Ikhlas: Chapter 112 of the Qur'an)

The whole creation with its manifold manifestations, so varied and yet so uniform, from the single leaf of a tree to the mighty stars and galaxies soaring in the sky, is proof of His existence, His love and His divine providence. Not only do we know about this Creator through the convincing evidence of how organized the universe is, but also through a line of prophets, including but not limited to Noah, Abraham, Moses, Jesus and Mohammed (peace be upon them all). They came to draw our attention to Him so that we may make the choice to believe by responding to our primordial worship-instinct and our God-gifted intellect that all that is organized must have an organizer and that this universe is the creation of the ultimate organizer

A Muslim faith is pronounced in the format of admitting the existence and oneness of the Creator as follows:

I witness that there is no God, but one God
and that Mohammed is His prophet.
(Or for that matter one of His prophets, since the Qur'an states that Mohammed is no more than a prophet and that a lot of prophets have passed before him).

WHAT ARE THE PILLARS OF ISLAM?

There are five major pillars of Islam which are the articles of faith. These pillars are (1) the belief (*Imaan*) in one God and that Muhammad (peace be upon him) is His messenger, (2) prayer (Salah) which is prescribed five times a day, (3) fasting (*Saw'm*) which is required in the month of Ramadan, (4) charity (*zakah*) which is the poor-due on the wealth of the rich and (5) *Hajj* which is the pilgrimage to Mecca once in a lifetime if one can afford it physically and financially. The five pillars of Islam are summarized in the following Prophetic tradition (*hadeeth*) of Prophet Muhammad (peace be upon him):

> *"Islam has been built upon five things – on testifying that there is no god save Allah, and that Muhammad is His Messenger; on performing salah; on giving the zakah; on Hajj to the House; and on fasting during Ramadan."* (Al-Bukhari & Muslim)

This book will have its main focus on the wisdoms behind the five pillars of Islam from a religious-scientific perspective. However, the five pillars of Islam are just the fundamental building blocks of the edifice of Islam. In order to complete the building of Islam and in order to be a Muslim, one should not only be practicing the pillars of Islam but also be observing the moral codes of Islam such as honesty, truthfulness, steadfastness and many other human moral qualities to be a good human being. One should also excel in optional faith-building acts such as optional fasting, early morning prayers, contemplating on the Qur'an, to name only a few. Only then the building will be complete and beautiful.

CHAPTER ONE

Wisdom behind Obligatory Prayers (*Salah*)

S*ALAH* OR PRAYERS IS THE FIRST and the foremost pillar of Islam. The first question asked on the Day of Judgment will be about "*salah*" or the obligatory prayers. *Salah* is the first act that the person will be held accountable for on the Day when everyone will be standing before their Lord for reckoning. Prophetic companion Abdullah bin Qart narrated that the Prophet Muhammad (peace be upon him) said in a *hadeeth* (Prophetic tradition): *"The first act that the man will be accountable for on the Day of Judgment will be prayer. If it is good, then the rest of his acts will be good. And if it is evil, then the rest of his acts will be evil."* (Tabarani)

Salah is the last thing that Prophet Muhammad (peace be upon him) recommended to his followers before he died, saying, *"Prayer, prayer and what your right hand possesses."* It will be the last thing taken away from the religion. When it perishes, Islam will perish. The Messenger of Allah (peace be upon him) said, *"If Islam were stripped away, piece by piece, people would hold tight to the next one. The first thing taken would be ruling and governance, and the last thing would be prayer."* (Related by Ibn Hibban from the *hadeeth* of Abu Umamah) The five obligatory prayers offered by Muslims are to be performed each day at the prescribed times – at dawn, at noon, in the afternoon, in the evening (just after sunset), and at night fall.

The importance of *salah* is so great that one is ordered to observe it while traveling or not, while one is safe or in fear, while one is healthy or sick. According to the Qur'an, forsaking the prayers was one of the reasons for the destruction of the nations prior to Islam. In this chapter, the philosophy and wisdom behind prayers and some of its scientific benefits will be discussed.

CURE FOR HEEDLESSNESS IN OFFERING *SALAH* FIVE TIMES A DAY

Salah is the most effective cure to the disease of heedlessness (*ghaflaa*) towards God. This cure has been prescribed by the Creator himself as stated in the Qur'an: *"Surely I am Allah, there is no god but I, therefore worship Me and establish regular prayer for My remembrance."* (Surah Ta-Ha: 14) Offering *salah* five times a day takes the heedlessness away. According to some Islamic scholars, the word "*Insaan*" (Arabic word for human being) came from the Arabic word "*nasa yansee*" which means, "to forget." The Qur'an testifies to this human weakness, which is ingrained in his very nature: *"We (Allah) gave a command to Adam before this, but he forgot it, and We did not find firmness of purpose in him."* (Surah Ta-Ha: 115) In explaining this Quranic verse, the famous commentator on the Qur'an, Abdullah bin Abbas stated:

> *"Indeed, man is called insaan because, having covenanted with Him, he forgot (nasiya)."*

Man is composed of forgetfulness, which is the cause of his disobedience to his Lord when he forgets to fulfill his duty. In order to remind them of their covenant with Allah and the purpose of their creation, Muslims have been prescribed with five compulsory (*fard*) prayers, which expand from before dawn until after dusk. In order to make the remembrance of the Almighty God a part of man's daily life, Islam has prescribed daily prayers. Through prayers, a person strives to bring his/her human soul in communion with its Creator.

When we are indulged in pursuit of worldly affairs in our everyday life, we weave a kind of veil around our hearts, a veil of heedlessness. Five times obligatory daily prayers serve to take off that spiritual veil from our hearts. Our hearts reorient themselves towards their Creator five times a day everyday by offering *salah*. Dr. Mohammad Iqbal, famous Muslim poet and philosopher, has aptly described this condition in his book *Reconstruction of Religious Thought in Islam* in the following words:

> *"The timing of the daily prayer which, according to the Qur'an*

restores 'self-possession' to the ego by bringing it into closer touch with the ultimate source of life and freedom, is intended to save the ego from the mechanizing effects of sleep and business. Prayer in Islam is the ego's escape from mechanism to freedom." [2]

The human body is made from ingredients of this world but soul (*rooh*) is blown into his body by an angel. The human body, therefore, possesses desires similar to those of animals whereas the human soul strives for the heavenly desires. The worship instinct is the desire of the human soul, whereas instincts for hunger, thirst, and sex are the desires of the body. The Qur'an tells us, *"Verily in the remembrance of Allah do hearts find rest."* (Surah Ar-Raad: 28) One form of this remembrance is *salah*, as mentioned elsewhere in the Qur'an: *"So worship Me and establish regular prayer for My remembrance."* (Surah Ta-Ha: 14) Hence, prayer is instinctive in its origin. Human nature finds comfort and solace only by worshipping and supplicating his/her Creator and Lord. Notable American psychologist William James sheds some light on this aspect of human personality in the following passage:

"It seems probable that in spite of all that science may do to the contrary, men will continue to pray to the end of time, unless their mental nature changes in a manner which nothing we know should lead us to expect.... Most men, either continually or occasionally, carry a reference to it in their breasts. The humblest outcast on this earth can feel himself to be real and valid by means of this higher recognition.... It is a much more essential part of the consciousness of some men than of others. Those who have the most of it are possibly the most religious men. But I am sure that even those who say that they are altogether without it deceive themselves, and really have it in some degree." [3]

---

[2] Iqbal, Sir Mohammad (Allama) (1994). *The Reconstruction of Religious Thought in Islam.* New Delhi, Kitaab Bhavan.

[3] James, William quoted in: Iqbal, Sir Mohammad (Allama) (1994). The Reconstruction of Religious Thought in Islam. New Delhi, Kitaab Bhavan.

SALAH– A SUMMATION OF ALL FORMS OF PRAYERS BY DIFFERENT CREATURES

Salah holds a distinction that it is a combination and culmination of all forms of prayer in the whole universe. The late Islamic researcher, Dr. Muhammad Hamidullah, noted that we can classify three types of things in the universe: (1) rocks and minerals, (2) animals, and (3) vegetation. Rocks cannot move but stay still. Similarly, Muslims stand still in prayers. Hence, we have the method of prayers of rocks incorporated in *salah*. Animals are always "in a state of genuflexion, bowing the head in humility."[4] Such is the prayer of animals. The Muslims observe the same when they bend their head in reverence during *salah*. The vegetation is in a state of prostration because trees have their roots deep in the earth. Muslims prostrate themselves during *salah* or prayer. This fact is alluded to in the Qur'an where is it said: *"The sun and the moon follow a reckoning, and the herbs and the trees all prostrate themselves."* (Surah Ar-Rahman: 5, 6)

In addition to combining the ways of rocks, animals, and vegetative life, *salah* contains certain features which are purely distinctive of human beings, e.g., salutation to God (al-tahiyyah) during the prayers.[5] This is understandable in light of the noble status granted by Allah to human beings over His other creations. In fact, the human nose and forehead have been created in such a way that they fit on the ground very well in the state of prostration. Thus, *salah* is a combination of all forms of prayer of the entire universe.

MEDICAL BENEFITS OF OFFERING *SALAH*

Although the basic purpose of obligatory prayers or *salah* is not to provide an exercise for people, yet if we looked from the scientific point of view, there are a multitude of medical benefits for the human body in

---

[4] Hamidullah, Dr. Mohammad (1992). *Introduction to Islam*. New Delhi, Kitab Bhavan.
[5] Hamidullah, Dr. Mohammad (1992). *Introduction to Islam*. New Delhi, Kitab Bhavan.

offering *salah* five times a day. In fact Prophet Muhammad (peace be upon him) mentioned in a tradition in Ibn Majah that prayer is a cure for many diseases. If we simply ponder over the distribution of their timings, we will notice that Allah has distributed the timings of the five obligatory prayers in such a way that those prayers which are offered with an empty stomach, i.e., *Fajr* (early morning *salah*), *Asr* (later afternoon *salah*), and *Maghrib* (after sunset *salah*), are short in terms of their *rak'ahs* (units). Conversely, for the prayers offered after the meals, i.e., *Dhuhar* (noon *salah*) and *Isha* (night *salah*), their collective rak'ahs are more and that is so that the body can get mild exercise after the meals. Similarly, taraweeh prayers (offered in the fasting month of Ramadan) are held after the event of breaking the fast because after the whole day of fasting, the human body is dumped with lots of food at the time of breaking the fast. In fact, Prophet Muhammad (peace be upon him) said in a *hadeeth*:

> *"Dissolve and digest your food by doing remembrance of Allah and by offering salah."* (narrated by Abu Nuaym)

In general, health aspects of *salah* can be classified into three categories:

(1) **Wudu:** Before prayer, Muslims perform ritual ablutions, known as wudu. The Islamic ritual of performing wudu consists of rinsing the face, hands, and feet with clean water – as a mark of respect to God. Rinsing all the exposed areas of the body (including hands, feet, face, mouth, nostrils, etc.) five times a day is a healthy preventive measure. We know today that hospitals, restaurants, and other places emphasize hand washing for their employees in order to prevent the spread of germs. Muslims were commanded to do so in the Qur'an (Surah Al-Ma'idah: 6) more than 1400 years ago.

Similarly, flushing out the nasal cavity by putting water in nostrils three times during every wudu has deep biological implications. We now know that many sinus sufferers turn to nasal saline irrigation for relief, a therapy that uses salt and water solution to flush out the nasal cavity. Chronic sinus problems comprise of headaches, facial pain and clogged nasal passages. Nasal irrigation is one of the ways to treat such symptoms.

In fact, the ear, nose, and throat (ENT) surgeons recommend nasal irrigation for their patients who have undergone sinus surgery, to clear away crusting in the nasal passages. Many patients with chronic sinus symptoms from bacterial infections, allergies, and environmental irritants also use different methods of nasal irrigation (such as using a Neti pot or other such devices) in order to alleviate congestion, facial pain and pressure, and reduce the need for antibiotics and nasal sprays.[6] Rinsing out the nostrils three times in every ablution before performing *salah* is an effective and healthy nasal irrigation technique.

(2) **Recitation of the Qur'an**: When the Qur'an is recited during the five daily prayers, it has a healing effect on the body and the heart. The Qur'an tells us: *"O mankind! There has come to you a good advice from your Lord (i.e., the Qur'an), and a healing for that (disease) in your breasts – a guidance and a mercy for the believers."* (Surah Yunus: 57)

The human body and heart are responsive to the recitation of the Qur'an. This has been shown by scientific experimentation separately by two Muslim scientists in two different parts of the world. One of the scientific studies was conducted in 1984 at the Akbar Clinics, Panama City in Florida in the United States of America by Dr. Ahmed Elkadi who used the most sophisticated and state-of-the-art instruments in his research. In those series of experiments conducted and published by Dr. Elkadi, the effects of listening to the Quranic recitation on physiological parameters, i.e., heart rate, blood pressure, and muscle tension, were monitored among three groups of volunteers – Muslims who understood Arabic, Muslims who did not understand Arabic, and non-Muslims who did not understand Arabic. The results of his study showed very clearly that listening to the recitation of the Qur'an resulted in relaxation of smooth muscles, reduction of heart rate, and all the physiological changes, which are all indicative of release from stress and anxiety. These effects were produced both among Muslims and non-Muslims, regardless of whether they understood the Arabic language or not.

---

[6] WebMD Medical Reference (2009) Reviewed by Jonathan L Gelfand, MD on June 13, 2009 (http://www.webmd.com/allergies/sinus-pain-pressure-9/neti-pots)

Another important observation reported was that, within the Qur'an itself, listening to recitation of the verses promising reward (verses of *Targheeb*) caused more stress-reducing effects (e.g., more tranquility in the heart rate) on the listeners, whereas listening to the recitation of the verses promising punishment (verses of Tarheeb) caused less stress-reducing effect on the listeners.[7] This study demonstrates the beneficial effects of recitation of the Qur'an on human body and heart.

A similar scientific study was carried out at the University of Khartoum, Sudan, by Dr. Muhammad Khair al-Irgisoosi during his Ph.D. research under the supervision of Dr. Malik Badri (world-renowned Islamic psychologist). The subjects of this study were patients suffering from hypertension due to stressful lifestyle or other reasons. The results of this study also showed that listening to the recitation of the Qur'an contributed significantly to lowering blood pressure among the patients.[8] These research findings support the results of research conducted at Akbar Clinics in the U.S.A. Needless to say, those effects of the Quranic recitation will only intensify during *salah*, which is a spiritual exercise, and when the person performing *salah* is already in a spiritually-receptive state.

(3) **Physical Exercise:** The movements in *salah* are mild, uniform, and involve all muscles and joints. The standing and bowing down in the prayers involves exercise of muscles and joints of the body. The caloric output helps keep energy balance in the body. Each rak'ah uses twenty calories.[9] In *salah*, a rak'ah is defined as a unit within a prayer which involves recitation while standing, bowing down once, and two prostrations.

---

[7] Elkadi, Ahmed Health and Healing in the Qur'an in Athar, Shahid, M.D., Ed. (1993). *Islamic Perspectives in Medicine - A Survey of Islamic Medicine: Achievements & Contemporary Issues.* Indianapolis, American Trust Publications.

[8] Badri, Malik (2000). *Contemplation: An Islamic Psychospiritual Study.* London, The International Institute of Islamic Thought.

[9] Athar, Shahid, M.D., Ed. (1993). *Islamic Perspectives in Medicine - A Survey of Islamic Medicine: Achievements & Contemporary Issues.* Indianapolis, American Trust Publications.

Among the components of *salah*, an important element is sajdah (the act of prostration) in which the forehead touches the ground. *Sajdah* or prostration is an act of worship which can be seen only among the Muslims today. This act of worship has practically almost disappeared from all the religions revealed prior to Islam. In the Qur'an, there has been mention of sajdah or prostration in more than 90 different places. In the Qur'an, human beings are commanded: *"Prostrate yourself and draw near to Allah."* (Surah Al-Alaq: 19) A person is closest to Allah while in the state of prostration as affirmed by a Prophetic tradition (*hadeeth*): *"The closest a slave ever is to his Lord is when he is in prostration, so make much supplication."* (Sahih Muslim) [10] During our everyday life, our brain is placed at a higher position than our heart but that sometimes results in the arrogance of our brain. However, when we prostrate to our Lord Allah, our heart attains a higher position in our body than our brain and that is the state of a human being in which he/she is closest to Allah as mentioned in this Prophetic tradition.

In one *hadeeth* (Prophetic tradition) narrated by Anas bin Malik, the Holy Prophet (peace be upon him) advised Muslims to perform ruku (bowing) and sajdah properly. In another *hadeeth*, he advised to perform sajdah and ruku (bowing) calmly and to get up only when the body has come to ease. From the medical point of view, when in a state of prostration, there is flowing of extra blood supply to the brain which provides extra-nourishment to the brain and it has wholesome effects on a person's memory, eyesight, hearing, mental concentration, and other mental abilities. According to medical doctor and Islamic researcher Dr. Zakir Naik, during prostration there is drainage of sinuses and, hence, fewer chances of a person getting sinusitis (inflammation of the sinuses). During the night's sleep, the breathing process is slowed, as a result of which only two-thirds of the capacity of the lung is exhaled; the remaining one third stays in the lungs as residual air. During prostration, the muscles beneath the lungs are pressed, and as a consequence, the remaining one-third

---

[10] Muslim, Imam Abul Hussain Qasheeri (1981). *Sahih Muslim*. Lahore, Khalid Ihsan Publishers.

residual air has the chance to be expelled, which is important for healthy lungs. In addition, accumulated mucus in the lungs has the chance to be drained from the lungs during prostration and a person has less chances of having diseases of the lungs such as bronchiolitis (swelling of the smallest air passages of the lungs). Similarly, in the state of prostration, there is increased venous return and, hence, there is less chance of having a hernia, etc. Furthermore, when we perform different acts of *salah*, i.e., standing up, bowing down, sitting with our legs folded, prostration (*qiyaam, ruku, tashahhud, sajdah*), and when we stand up from the same position, the weight is localized on the bottom of the feet. The calf muscles and the thigh muscles are activated. This results in increased blood supply to the lower part of the body, which strengthens our legs. Moreover, when we do various postures like standing erect, bowing down, prostrating, the vertebral column takes various postures, and there is less chance of having a disease of the vertebra or the spine.[11]

There are myriads of other benefits of sajdah. In the words of Dr. Karim Beebani, a medical practitioner, the position of sajdah can be considered as a "mini dive" as the person performing *salah* puts his/her forehead on the ground while his hands are placed at the sides, which "brings most of the body muscles if not all in active motion and serves to give them some exercise."[12] Commenting on the various medical benefits of prostration in *salah*, Dr. Beebani continues:

"In the unique position of *Sajdah*, the neck muscles get the best exercise. They have to bear the load when the forehead lies at the ground; hence, the neck muscles become stronger. One can note the tense pressure at the neck muscles in the position of *Sajdah* specially the active motion of the neck and the facial muscles when the head is being lifted (e.g., one inch above the ground) and it will be noticed that they are in a very active motion.

[11] Discover Islam TV Series "The Daily Prayer (Medical Benefit of Prayer)" Dr. Zakir Naik interviewed by Dr. Linda Thayer
[12] Beebani, Dr. Muhammad Karim [Saudi Gazette] (July 7, 2000). "The Medical Benefits of Sajdah." The Muslim World.

Stronger cervical muscles mean the cervical vertebra will be better protected. Strength of cervical muscles is important as the head rests upon cervical vertebra supported by cervical musculature. In fact, the head performs rotator movements over the cervical vertebra. In any accident cervical neck examination is especially important to the physicians because of its extraordinary importance. It is uncommon that a person who offers his prayers regularly will get the usual neck myalgias [muscle pain] or cervical spondylosis as the neck muscles particularly become very strong due to the 34 sajdahs offered daily in five prayers… Holy Prophet Muhammad (peace be upon him) used to elongate the position of Ruku (bending) and Sajdah positions and he advised to do so. In the light of the above facts it is appropriate to say that from medical point of view as well this advice is a golden rule for health." [13]

Finally, it must be reminded that Muslims offer *salah* to thank Allah and to obey His commandment. *Salah* is not meant to be an exercise. However there are a multitude of medical advantages associated with it as there are wisdoms and benefits in every commandment in Islam.

CONGREGATIONAL PRAYERS AND THE HUMAN HEART

Muslim men have been commanded in the Qur'an and Prophetic traditions to perform five times daily prayers in congregation. Each prayer in congregation is equivalent to performing 27 prayers individually (Sahih Bukhari & Muslim). [14] This command pertains to Muslim men while Muslim women are exempt from performing prayers in the mosque due to their responsibilities at their homes. The blessings of congregational prayers can be easily understood from an interesting research described by American intellectual Joseph Chilton Pearce in his book *The Biology of Transcendence*. Pearce notes that if a single heart cell is placed on a slide in a laboratory and observed under a microscope, we observe that the single heart cell keeps on beating for a short time, then it loses its

[13] Ibid.
[14] Bukhari, Imam Abu Abdullah Mohammad bin Ismael (1981). *Sahih Bukhari*. Lahore, Khalid Ihsan.

rhythm, becomes weak and eventually dies. Now if we place two heart cells on a slide and keep them at a very far distance, they also die after a short time of beating without rhythm. But, if we take two heart cells and put them close together on a slide (they do not need to touch each other), we will be surprised to see that the two heart cells start to beat in synchrony (with the same rhythm) and they do not die. The same phenomenon occurs at a larger scale in the case of a complete heart. All the heart cells beat in synchrony (with the same rhythm in unity), which makes the heart such a powerful organ.

What is the reason behind the synchronous beating of the two heart cells (even though they are not connected to each other), which prevents them from dying? Since the heart has billions of small cells pulsating in unity, they produce electrical energy forming an electromagnetic field. According to Joseph Pearce, when the electromagnetic waves produced by the two heart cells on a slide match (synchronize), the two heart cells strengthen each other and start to beat in unity.[15] This phenomenon can be observed at the macroscopic (grand) level as well. When people are in close proximity in a room, their hearts start to beat with the same rhythm. Even their breathing pattern synchronizes in such instances.

From the above-mentioned research about the heart cells, the wisdom behind an important commandment of Prophet Muhammad (peace be upon him) about the power of congregational prayers and straightening the rows in the congregational prayers can be understood. No'man bin Bashir narrates a tradition from Prophet Muhammad (peace be upon him) according to which the Prophet used to tell his companions before the prayers

"Straighten your rows three times. Otherwise, Allah will make your hearts turn against each other." (Sunan Abu Dawud)[16]

---

[15] Pearce, Joseph Chilton (2002). *The Biology of Transcendence.* Rochester, Vermont, Park Street Press.
[16] Abu Dawud, Imam Sulayman bin Ash'as Sajastani (1983). *Sunan Abu Dawud.* Lahore, Islamic Academy Urdu Bazaar.

Biophysicists have discovered that the heart generates a very strong electromagnetic field that can be measured with instruments such as magnetometers from a distance of up to ten feet away. The electromagnetic field produced by the heart encompasses the whole body. In fact, it is so powerful that we can take an electrocardiogram reading from as far as three feet away from the body. Research has also shown that when people are in close proximity, the electromagnetic energy produced by their hearts is exchanged between the people and this energy exchange can be detected with sensitive instruments. [17]

In addition, the heart cells undergo the phenomenon of "entrainment" similar to pendulums. A European scientist named Christiaan Huygens discovered this phenomenon in the 17th century. When we have many pendulums swinging together in a room, no matter how different they are at the start of swinging, soon all the pendulums start to swing with the same rhythm as that of the largest pendulum because it has the largest and strongest rhythm. This phenomenon is found in biological systems as well. Hearts also generate waves when they beat (since they are the largest oscillators in the body). This means that all the hearts start to be affected by waves generated by the strongest heart (which could be sometimes the heart of the leader or Imam – the person leading the prayers) and start to beat in the same rhythm (pulled into entrainment) as that of the strongest heart. [18]

When Muslims are praying behind one Imam and they straighten their rows, their hearts become synchronized as a result. Their hearts beat in unity and, thus, their hearts are strengthened. In one *hadeeth*, Abu Mas'ud reported: *"The Messenger of Allah (peace be upon him) used to touch our shoulders in prayer and say: Keep straight, don't be irregular, otherwise your hearts will be disunited."* (*Sahih Muslim*) The Holy Prophet (peace be

[17] McCraty, R. (PhD), Atkinson, M., Tomasino, D. (BA) & Tiller, W.A. (PhD) The Electricity of Touch: Detection and measurement of cardiac energy exchange between people. In: Pribram, K.H. Ed. (1998). *Brain and Values: Is a Biological Science of Values Possible*. Mahwah, NJ, Lawrence Erlbaum Associates: pp. 359-379.
[18] Childre, Doc & Martin, Howard (1999). *The HeartMath Solution*. New York, HarperSanFrancisco.

upon him) emphasized that if Muslims saying the prayers do not keep their rows straight, their hearts will not beat in synchrony, and hence, they will not be united. The Prophet (peace be upon him) stressed it so much that according to a narration of Waabisa bin Ma'bad, when Prophet Muhammad (peace be upon him) saw a man who was saying prayers alone behind the rows, he commanded the man to repeat his prayers. (*Tirmidhi*)

DIVINE PROMISE OF PROVISION FOR THOSE WHO OFFER SALAH REGULARLY

Allah the Exalted One tells us the following about *salah* in the Qur'an:

"Enjoin salah on your household, and do keep observing it. We do not ask you for any worldly provision; rather, it is We Who provide you. The ultimate end is for piety." (Surah Taha: 132)

This verse of the Qur'an suggests a Divine promise of provision for those who offer *salah* and remain steadfast on it. Contemporary commentator on the Qur'an, Sheikh Amin Ahsan Islaahi, writes in explaining this Quranic verse:

"Allah is saying that We are responsible for providing you with sustenance. You should do the job which We have ordained on you and leave the rest on Us. Do not worry about your sustenance. In the words of Prophet Jesus (peace be upon him): 'As long as the laborer is performing his duty, he deserves his earnings.'" (Tafseer Tadabbarul Qur'an, vol. 5)

For this reason, it is extremely important for all the adult family members especially the head of a family to be punctual and steadfast in saying *salah*. When the head of a family becomes negligent in his prayers, the whole family suffers the consequences. *Barakahs* (Divine blessings) are taken away from the earnings of that house.

EFFECTS OF *SALAH* ON THE SOCIETY

In the Qur'an, Allah the Exalted One tells us the following about *salah*:

"And establish regular Prayer: for Prayer restrains from shameful and unjust deeds." (Surah Al-Ankabut: 45)

The Qur'an has described this quality of *salah* that it restrains a person from committing evil deeds. In fact, there is no other form of worship better than *salah* for moral training of a person. A person performing *salah* has to stand before God five times a day, every day. This refreshes in one's mind the concept of accountability before Allah the Almighty. Daily standing in *salah* accentuates in one's mind that Allah is aware of a person's inward intentions and outward actions. It is for this reason when any non-practicing Muslim turns towards religion, the very first thing he/she begins to do is to say prayers five times a day. Regularity in offering *salah* results in moral training of a person, which in turn has positive effects on the society. People who offer *salah* regularly do a better job in terms of enjoying the good and forbidding the evil (*amr bil ma'ruf wa nahee anil munkar*) in the society. In this context, the saying of Imam Jaafar as-Saadiq must be remembered when he said: "If a person would like to know if the Lord has accepted his prayers, let him see if *salah* has stopped him from committing evil and indecent acts. If *salah* has prevented him from committing the sinful acts, this means his *salah* has been accepted by Allah." (*Tafseer Rooh al-Ma'anee*)

Congregational *salah* teaches the Muslims that collective benefits of the society are more important than individual benefits so that a person should not become egocentric. The culmination of the social aspect of *salah* is seen every Friday at the time of *salah al-Jumuah* (Friday prayers) when Muslims from far off places come and perform *salah* behind one Imam. This scene of Muslim unity is so mesmerizing that many non-Muslims accepted Islam just when they saw so many Muslims bowing down and prostrating together behind one Imam who is leading the prayers.

Psychologically, all levels within the society are eradicated when people are performing the *salah*. In *salah*, a prince and pauper, an employer and an employee, and a landlord and a peasant stand shoulder to shoulder, bow down and prostrate to the Almighty Allah. By doing so, Islam gives a lesson to humanity that all human beings are created equal and that no one should oppress the other.

In his thought-provoking book *Lost Boys*, American clinical psychologist Dr. James Garbarino has quoted the social scientific research of psychologist Andrew Weaver from America's University of Hawaii. In this research, Dr. Weaver found out that in a society where majority of the young people are inclined to religion and spirituality, there are lesser crimes among the youth of that society compared to a society with its youth with lesser interest in the religion. According to Dr. Weaver, such surveys reveal that religion and spirituality are highly valuable to many people in times of crisis, trauma, and grief. Prayers help people in coping with trauma and crisis. [19] There is no doubt that *salah*, especially congregational *salah*, prevents Muslim youth from indulging in sins. Therefore, Muslim parents ought to encourage their Muslim youth to offer *salah* regularly.

EXAMPLES OF THOSE WHO LOVED *SALAH*

Islamic history is filled with the examples of those who would sink deep into the love of Allah when they used to offer *salah*. Here just a few examples will be given.

Prophet Muhammad (peace be upon him) used to offer shorter prayers when he was leading people while he used to offer longer prayers when he would perform *salah* alone. (Musnad Ahmed, Nisai) Muslim scholar Ibn Hajar Al-Asqalani states that Prophet Muhammad (peace be upon him) used to offer shorter rak'ahs when in congregation so that people who were being lead by him in prayers would not feel any discomfort. However, he would offer long prayers when he was alone because in prayers there was coolness to his eyes. Sometimes, his feet would be swollen due to prolonged standing in the prayers. His companions

---

[19] Garbarino, James (1999). *Lost Boys*. New York, Free Press (Simon & Schuster, Inc.).

used to ask him, *"O Prophet of Allah! Why do you do this while Allah has forgiven all your sins?"* Prophet Muhammad *(peace be upon him) would reply, "Should I not become a grateful slave of Allah."* (Bukhari; Muslim)

The Prophet's companion and first caliph Abu Bakr As-Siddique used to spend a whole night saying prayers, and he would stand still like a stick fixed on the ground. He used to weep a lot while performing the prayers.

Imam Sha'raani (Islamic historian and traditionist) stated that when Umar bin Khattab was elected as the second caliph of the Muslims, he stopped sleeping during the day as well as night. He would only take short naps. He used to say that if I sleep during the day, it will result in the loss of my subjects, and if I sleep during the night (instead of performing optional *salah*), it will be the loss of my life in the Hereafter.

It is narrated about the cousin of the Prophet, Ali bin Abi Talib, that when an arrow would penetrate in his body in a war, the physicians could only take it out of his body while he was in prayers because that was the time when he used to be completely immersed in worship and would not feel any pain.

Another of the Prophet's companion, Abu Talha was once performing *salah* in his huge garden filled with fruit trees. All of a sudden, a bird lost its way in the garden. Abu Talha began looking at the bird while he was performing *salah* and forgot at what stage he was in the prayers. He became very sad at the end of his prayers that he could not maintain his concentration in prayers due to his beautiful garden. He gave his whole garden as charity in the path of Allah.

It is narrated that it was the habit of Raabia Basaria, famous woman Islamic scholar, to keep her coffin in front of her while she used to perform *salah* to remember her death. Often her place of prostration would become wet because of her tears in love of Allah.

CHAPTER TWO

Wisdom and Scientific Benefits of Fasting (*Saw'm*)

R AMADAN IS THE NINTH MONTH OF the Islamic calendar. It has been prescribed upon Muslims to fast in this month, and it is one of the five pillars of Islam. Muslims all over the world observe total fasting (no food or water) between dawn and sunset in the month of Ramadan. They do so not for any medical benefits but only to obey the commandment of Allah as it is mentioned in the Qur'an: *"O you who believe! Fasting is prescribed to you, as it was prescribed for those before you (i.e., Jews and Christians) so that you may become the Muttaqun (the pious)."* (Surah Al-Baqarah: 183) In addition, there are also voluntary fasts in other months of the lunar Islamic calendar, which Muslims are encouraged to observe.

The word "*saw'm*" means to abstain from something. In the Islamic commandments, "*saw'm*" or fasting means to abstain from drinking, eating and sexual relations with one's spouse from before sunrise until sunset. There are various Prophetic traditions about the rewards of fasting.

The Prophet (peace be upon him) said, *"Allah said: The fast is for Me, and I will give the reward for it, as he (the one who observes the fast) leaves his sexual desire, food and drink for My Sake. Fasting is a screen (from Hell), and there are two pleasures (moments of happiness or joys) for a fasting person, one at the time of breaking his fast, and the other at the time when he will meet his Lord. And the smell of the mouth of a fasting person is better in Allah's Sight than the smell of musk."* (Bukhari)

Abdullah ibn Amr reported that the Messenger of Allah (peace be upon him) said: "The fast and the Qur'an are two intercessors for the servant of Allah on the Day of Resurrection. The fast will say: *'O Lord, I prevented him from his food and desires during the day. Let me intercede for* him.' The Qur'an will say: 'I prevented him from sleeping at night. Let me intercede for him.' And their intercession will be accepted." (Musnad Ahmad)

Abu Hurairah reported that the Prophet (peace be upon him) said: *"There are three people whose supplications are not rejected: the fasting person when he breaks the fast, the just ruler and the supplication of the oppressed."* (Tirmidhi, Ibn Majah and Ibn Hibban)

Abu Umamah reported: *"I came to the Messenger of Allah and said: 'Order me to do a deed that will allow me to enter Paradise.' He said: 'Stick to fasting, as there is no equivalent to it.' Then I came to him again and he said: 'Stick to fasting.'"* (Ibn Hibban, an-Nisa'i, and al-Hakim: Sahih)

Sahl ibn Sa'd reported that the Prophet (peace be upon him) said: *"There is a gate to Paradise that is called ar-Rayyan. On the Day of Resurrection it will say: 'Where are those who fasted?' When the last [one] has passed through the gate, it will be locked."* (Bukhari and Muslim)

According to the Islamic scholar Izz ud din bin Abdussalaam, the whole purpose of every injunction of Islam is to remove harm and to benefit humanity (*jalbul masaalih wa dar ul mafasid*). Therefore, Allah has placed myriads of benefits in fasting for human beings. In this chapter, the wisdom and benefits of fasting will be discussed in light of the Qur'an, sunnah and modern science.

FASTING AS A TRAINING OF SELF-CONTROL

According to psychologists, the two strongest desires human beings possess are the desire to eat and drink. If a person can control these desires, he will be able to control most of his desires. It is precisely these urges Muslims are required to control during fasting. Psychologists also tell us that if we do something for three weeks continuously, it becomes a permanent habit. Fasting for four weeks during the month of Ramadan gives a person a complete training in self-discipline. It is for this reason that many Muslims who have previously been living sinful lives, after passing through one-month training of Ramadan, become successful in creating the necessary will-power and motivation to sincerely repent and change their lives for better. Egyptian Muslim psychologist Muhammad Usman Najati states in this book *Qur'an and Psychology* (Arabic title: *Qur'an wa Ilm un Nafs*):

> "The continuous practice of controlling our carnal desires for a whole month every year creates will-power in a person not only to control his body demands but also to fulfill our religious responsibilities and to spend the whole life in accordance with the commandments of Allah." [20]

Renowned contemporary Muslim psychologist Dr. Malik Badri carried out a study for the World Health Organization (WHO) on the alcohol abusers in Sudan, which was presented in the first annual meeting of *"Promotion and Development of Traditional Medicine,"* held in Geneva in the year 1978. In this study, Dr. Badri found that almost all the alcohol-drinking subjects of his study were able to abstain from their habit of drinking during Ramadan, although some of the subjects took alcohol during the first few nights of Ramadan to escape the withdrawal symptoms. By the end of Ramadan, many of them felt enough spirituality in them that they took an oath on the Qur'an never to go back to drinking alcohol. Dr. Badri followed the subjects of his study many years later and still found them firm on their repentance. [21]

The psychological effects of Ramadan fasting can be noticed among all Muslims. Police records in Muslim countries show a significant decline in the incidents of theft, murder, rape, car accidents, drunken aggression, etc. during the month of Ramadan as compared to the rest of the eleven months of the calendar, bearing testimony to the fact that feelings of peace and tranquility become prevalent among the fasting Muslims.

Fasting serves as training in patience and steadfastness. Fasting prevents our energies from being wasted and channels them in a constructive direction. As a consequence of fasting for a whole month, a

[20] Najati, Mohammad Usman (n.d.). *Qur'an wa Ilm un Nafs*. Lahore, Al-Faisal Publishers & Traders.
[21] Badri, Malik (1997). *The AIDS Crisis: An Islamic Socio-Culture Perspective*. Kuala Lumpur, International Institute of Islamic Thought & Civilization.

person gains self-control, patience, steadfastness, and God-consciousness. A person is prohibited certain otherwise permissible things during fasting so that, on the psychological level, it becomes easier for that person to quit and stay away from things prohibited in the religion. Ordinarily, a person's heart yearns for the best food. Human self has a yen to take rest in the bed for long hours. A person also has sexual desires. However, in a state of fasting, a person is prohibited to eat except at specified times. A person has to sacrifice his sleep when he/she gets up in the morning for suhoor (to eat something and begin the fast). A person is not allowed to have sexual relations with his wife during the fasting hours. Hence, the human self is trained to obey the restrictions so that it becomes easier for it to obey its Creator.

SCIENTIFIC RESEARCH ON FASTING

There are various medical and physiological benefits of fasting. Western researcher Allan Cott notes in his book *Fasting as a Way of Life:* "Fasting brings a wholesome physiological rest for the digestive tract and central nervous system and normalizes metabolism."[22] According to Dr. Shanti B. Rangwani of India, fasting helps in the clearance of toxins f rom the body. As no new food goes into the body during fasting, no new toxins are produced from the food, and the liver works "full time" to elim-inate those already existing toxins. This happens due to the fact that our body needs fuel for its survival, and when there is no new food in the body, it begins to first burn the toxins present in the body and then turns to the stored nutrients. As a consequence, the blood becomes purer, and the skin begins to acquire a new glow.[23] In light of this research, we can easily understand the *hadeeth* of Prophet Muhammad (peace be upon him) in which he said: "*For everything that you own there is zakah (obliga-tory charity), and zakah of your body is fasting.*" (Sunan Ibn Majah) *Zakah*

---

[22] Cott, Allan (1977). *Fasting as a Way of Life.* New York, Bantam Books. Quoted in: Athar, Shahid (M.D.) editor "Medical Aspects of Islamic Fasting" in Islamic Medicine (www.islam-use.com)
[23] Rangwani, Shanti B. (December 1998). "The Miracles of Fasting." In Comparative Religion The Islamic Voice 12-12 (144)

purifies a person's wealth of the impurities. Similarly, fasting purifies the body of the impurities and toxins. James Balch, M.D. writes in his book *Prescription for Nutritional Healing*: "Relieved of the work of digesting foods, fasting permits the body to rid itself of toxins while facilitating healing. Fasting regularly gives your organs a rest and helps reverse the ageing process for a longer and healthier life."[24]

It is interesting to note that fasting has no harmful effects whatsoever on the human body. Dr. Soliman of the University Hospital of Amman (Jordan) conducted a study on healthy volunteers during the month of Ramadan (1404 Hijra). There were 42 men and 26 women (in the age ranges of 15 to 64 years) who were being studied. Their body weights were recorded at the beginning and end of Ramadan and their blood was tested for the levels of cortisol, testosterone (sex hormone), glucose, total cholesterol, urea, etc. The results of the study revealed that there was a significant loss in weight in males and females (up to 2 kg) whereas the blood glucose level actually rose. All the other parameters did not show any significant changes.[25]

Another study was carried out at the University of Medical Sciences, Tehran (Iran), by Dr. F. Azizi and his associates and it was published in the Journal of Islamic Medical Association in 1987. In this study, nine healthy volunteer men were studied. Their blood was analyzed for the serum levels of glucose, bilirubin, calcium, phosphorous, protein, albumin, etc. before Ramadan as well as on the 10th, 20th, and 29th day of Ramadan. It was noted in the results of the study that intermittent abstinence from food and drink for 17 hours a day for 29 days does not alter male reproductive hormones or metabolism hormones.[26] Hence, it can be

[24] Balch, James (2000). *Prescription for Natural Healing.* Prentice Hall.
[25] Soliman, N. (Nov 1987). "The Effects of Fasting During Ramadan." *Journal of Islamic Medical Association.* Quoted in: Athar, Shahid (M.D.) editor "Medical Aspects of Islamic Fasting" in Islamic Medicine (www.islam-use.com)
[26] Azizi, F, et al. (Nov 1987). "Evaluation of Certain Hormones And Blood Constituents During Islamic Fasting Month." *Journal of Islamic Medical Association.* Quoted in: Athar, Shahid (M.D.) editor "Medical Aspects of Islamic Fasting" in *Islamic Medicine* (www.islam-use.com)

concluded from the above two studies that fasting has no adverse medical effects on the body, and it may have some beneficial effect on weight and lipid metabolism.

One of the benefits of fasting is that it strengthens the immune system of our body. A study published over two decades ago noted that famine victims in Africa were less likely to develop malaria and TB than their better-fed counterparts in refugee camps.[27] Fasting may also reverse the aging process considerably. In research studies exploring longevity on laboratory animals, it has been demonstrated that restriction of caloric intake increases longevity, slows the rate of functional decline, and reduces incidence of age-related disease in a variety of species. Although the mechanism of action of caloric restriction is not clear, it could perhaps be due to alteration in cellular functions in such a way that destructive by-products of metabolism are reduced, and defense or repair systems are enhanced by this nutritional manipulation.[28]

In this context, research was published in the February 1996 issue of the monthly *Ahlan Wasahlan* (Saudi Arabia), which was carried out by Dr. Usama Qandil at the Medical School of the prestigious Harvard University. In this research, Dr. Qandil and his associate scientists compared the influences of fasting on the immune systems of cancer patients suffering from immune deficiency.[29] In one group, he compared the natural killer-cell count in their bodies and their efficiency in attacking cancer cells just before the group embarked on fasting, as compared with their efficiency on the twenty-first day of Ramadan, and the twenty-eighth day of the month. The results were remarkable. Fasting greatly increased the number and activity of these killer cells in those fasting patients. Dr. Qandil also carefully compared the ratio of other defense cells of the immune system in both healthy and immune subjects includ-

[27] Rangwani, Shanti B (Dr.). (December 1998). "The Miracles of Fasting." In Comparative Religion. *The Islamic Voice* 12-12 (144)

[28] Syed, Ibrahim B. (Dr.). (December 1998). "Ramadan Fasting: Scientific Perspective." *The Islamic Voice* 12-12 (144)

[29] Qandil, Usama. (February 1996). *Ahlan Wasahlan* (Saudi monthly magazine) pg. 73

ing a sample of those who fasted in the month of Ramadan and those who did not. It is surprising to note that he observed a sudden increase in the number of T-cells, and this happened only in those who fasted. And of these cells, the helper T-cells had the highest increase. It must be noted that helper T-cells are the most important group of cells in the defense system of the human body because they act like the army general and control other cells of the immune system and organize the battle against invading germs. The AIDS virus and its collaborators are a killer because they target these T-cells. Hence, fasting enhances the defense system of the human body to better fight germs.[30]

Fasting overhauls and rejuvenates the body and gives it new strength. This phenomenon of rejuvenation through fasting can be observed in other creatures in nature. Dr. Geoffrey, a non-Muslim European, has made interesting observations regarding this matter in his book *Fasting* (published in Paris). He argues in his book that fasting is observed not only by human beings but by all creatures in nature, including animals and trees. Wild animals in the regions of heavy snowfall go without food for weeks and months and they still survive. This process is known as hibernation. Similarly, snakes hibernate during winter. This state of abstention from food and drink, i.e., the state of fasting, results in rejuvenation and renewal of life. Hibernating animals shed their old skin or feathers, and the new ones are fresher and better, hence experiencing a new youth. Fasting gives them greater strength and vigor. Similarly, trees shed their leaves during winter when they are not watered. They are in a state of fast, and this condition lasts for weeks or months. At the end of their fasting season, new leaves sprout forth, fresh flowers bloom and the trees bear fruit. In light of this evidence, Dr. Geoffrey argues that fasting is good for human beings. It helps give them health, renewed vigor, beauty, and virility. At the end of his book, the author suggests that every year people must fast for about forty days. It is interesting to note that when we add the 6 days of Shawwal fasts to the 30 days of Ramadan fasts, they

---

[30] Badri, Malik (1997). *The AIDS Crisis: An Islamic Socio-Culture Perspective.* Kuala Lumpur, International Institute of Islamic Thought & Civilization.

come out to be 36. The wisdom of fasting for about 40 days as it has now been understood by Dr. Geoffrey was known to Muslims for more than 1400 years.

LEARNING MODERATION IN EATING HABITS THROUGH FASTING

Fasting teaches us self-restraint so that we can observe moderation in our eating habits. Overeating is the cause of many diseases and health problems. According to the National Institute of Health (NIH), more that 80% of the diseases in the U.S. are related to diet intake.

Prophet Muhammad (peace be upon him) disliked excessive eating. He lived his whole life with a flat belly, and he died with a flat belly. Once he said:

> "We are a people who do not eat until we are hungry, and when we eat we do not eat our fill." (Related from 'Umar bin al-Khaṭṭāb.) [31]

It is important to exercise moderation in our eating habits. The consumption of small amounts of food assures tenderness of the heart, strength of the intellect, humility of the self and weakness of desires. Immoderate eating brings about the opposite of these praiseworthy qualities. Benjamin Franklin rightly said: "To lengthen thy life, lessen thy meals." This concept of "lessen thy meals" is ingrained in fasting. Ibrahim ibn Adham, a Muslim scholar, said: "Any one who controls his stomach is in control of his religion (deen), and anyone who controls his hunger is in control of good behavior. Disobedience towards Allah is nearest to a person who is satiated with a full stomach, and furthest away from a person who is hungry."

In another tradition, Prophet Muhammad (peace be upon him) said:

> *"No man fills a vessel worse than his stomach. A few morsels are enough for son of Adam (human being) to keep his back upright. But if he must eat more, then he should fill one third of his stomach with food, one third with drink and leave one third empty for the air (for easy breathing)."* (Reported by At-Tirmidhi)

[31] Ibn Katheer says its chain is weak, but the meaning is true

Those words were uttered by our Holy Prophet (peace be upon him) about 1400 years ago. Today, the science of human anatomy has informed us that the anterior end of the stomach is located just beneath the diaphragm, the major muscle responsible for the movement of lungs and breathing. Therefore, when we stuff our stomach with food, the diaphragm has difficulty in contracting and relaxing, resulting in a person having a hard time trying to breathe. The wisdom behind this Prophetic saying has been understood only today with the knowledge of science. In short, fasting teaches us to control our desire to eat and drink and, hence, to learn to practice moderation in our eating habits.

RAMADAN AND THE ISLAMIC PHILOSOPHY OF GOOD & EVIL

Religions before Islam also had the concept of fasting in them (as mentioned in Surah Al-Baqarah: 183). However, fasting in some religions involved eating only fruits during fasting, whereas in other religions it was limited to avoiding the eating of meals cooked on fire. Some religions had the permission of drinking only milk during fasting, while others had the authorization of drinking only water during fasting hours. In addition, in all the previous religions, the idea of fasting was more of penitence than of abstinence. Since Islam is a universal religion, the concept of fasting in Islam is much broader than any other religion. Islam commands its followers to have complete abstinence from eating or drinking from sunrise to sunset. This, in reality, is in accordance with the Islamic philosophy of good and evil, i.e., nip the evil in the bud. Islam does not leave loopholes and back doors in its commandments for the prohibited acts to enter. This is obvious in every Islamic teaching. For example, "*aab*" (father) was one of the names of Allah in almost all the micro (primitive) religions, as well as in Christianity and Judaism. However, Prophet Muhammad (peace be upon him) abrogated that name of Allah for us to call upon in our prayers. The reason is quite obvious. Polytheism (*shirk*) and anthropomorphism crept into the creed of Christianity through this door. The Christian theologians made Jesus the son of God. It was the same case with gambling. Other religions were lenient regarding gambling. Today, gambling is done in the premises of the churches under the name of 'bingo'. Music is also prohibited for the same reasons. With the exclusion of Islam, music entered almost all other religions of the world at their inception in the form of classical music. Today, music and dancing are performed inside churches and Hindu temples in the name of religion. The Islamic approach of nipping the evil in the bud can also be seen in commandments of the Qur'an not to go even close to *zina* (fornication) and the means and routes to fornication (*Surah Israa: 32*). Similarly, alcohol is *haram* (prohibited) in Islam, whether a person takes a sip or drinks a whole glass.

In other religions, it was permitted to eat or drink something during fasting (or at a later point in history the permission was introduced into the religion for general ease of the public). Therefore, fasting lost its value in those religions with the passage of time. Conversely, complete abstinence from eating and drinking in Islamic fasting has made it the only serious form of worship among the different forms of fasting of other religions.

RELATIONSHIP OF RAMADAN AND QUR'AN

Human beings are comprised of two things: (1) dust, and (2) spirit. Our whole life on this earth is in reality a story of conflict between our spiritual and material beings. This struggle ends upon our death when the spirit leaves the body. This is against the Western Darwinian concept of human beings. American humanist psychologist Abraham Maslow divided the basic needs of human beings into five "levels" in his famous Maslow's Pyramid. In that pyramid, the most basic need was for physiological survival, i.e., shelter, warmth, food, drink, and so on. Once those needs are met, the person can address his higher needs such as need for security, love, self-esteem. His pyramid gained fame in Western science because it is based on the Darwinian concept that human beings are like animals in every respect. Maslow's discovery is only half-true. He did not include a very basic need of human beings for their survival, i.e., the need to worship the Creator – the worship instinct. Indeed, the worship instinct is the quality of the human soul, and secular Western science completely denies the existence of the human soul.

It is mentioned in the Qur'an at various places that our body is made from the soil of this earth. For example, "And among His signs is that He created you from dust." (Surah Rome: 20) Our physical body came from this world and it will return back to this world:

'Thereof (the earth) We created you, and into it We shall return you, and from it We shall bring you out once again.' (Surah Ta-Ha: 55)

To this material being, Allah sends an angel to blow the spirit (rooh) into, as mentioned in the Qur'an: *"So when I have fashioned him and breathed into him (his) soul created by Me. then you (angels) fall down prostrate to him."* (Surah Saad: 72) The human soul (rooh) will return to Allah as mentioned in the Quranic verse: *'Truly! To Allah we belong, and truly to Him we shall return.'* (Surah Al-Baqarah: 156)

This angelic soul blown into human beings is unique among humans, and they do not share it with other living creatures on this planet. Thus, the human body is made from the ingredients of this world, but the soul is blown into the human body by an angel. Therefore, there is a body-soul conflict that happens inside a human being. The human body possesses desires similar to those of animals, whereas the human soul strives for heavenly desires.

The worship instinct is the desire of the human soul, whereas instincts for hunger, thirst, and sex are the desires of the body. The purpose of fasting is to curtail our carnal element and accentuate our angelic element. Ramadan is the month to provide nourishment to the human soul. All the ingredients of food for our physical body come from the soil of this earth because our physical being originated from this earth. However, our soul was blown into our body by an angel – a heavenly being. Therefore, its food must be something from the Heavens. In fact, the food for our soul is the heavenly revelation, Qur'an, which is the book of Allah. The Qur'an is the spring of life for our soul.

There is a profound relationship between Ramadan and Qur'an. Allah selected the month of Ramadan for the revelation of the Qur'an. The first revelation of the Qur'an was revealed to Prophet Muhammad (peace be upon him) when he was doing his i'tekaaf (spiritual retreat) in the cave of Hira. It has been mentioned in various traditions that during the month of Ramadan, Angel Jibreel used to visit Prophet Muhammad (peace be upon him) every night to read the Qur'an with him.

Hence, our physical body is catered to during the remaining eleven months, whereas in the month of Ramadan our soul is provided the opportunity for thirst quenching and nourishment. This food for our soul comes from recitation of the Qur'an, taraweeh (night) prayers, establishing nawaafil (supererogatory) prayers, contemplation on the meanings of the Holy Qur'an, etc., all of which provide a jumpstart to our soul for the rest of the eleven months.

AVOIDING THE THINGS WHICH POLLUTE FASTING

It is mentioned in a Prophetic tradition: *"Fasting is a shield (or screen). Let no one who is fasting commit any obscenity or foolishness. Should anyone engage him in a fight or abuse him, let him answer him by saying: 'I am fasting, I am fasting.'"* (Sahih Bukhari)

A fasting person gains the benefits of fasting only by avoiding the things which pollute his/her fast because otherwise he/she gets nothing else out of fasting except to remain hungry and thirsty. It has been narrated by Abu Huraira that Prophet Muhammad (peace be upon him) said: *"Whoever does not give up forged speech and evil actions, Allah is not in need of his leaving his food and drink (i.e., Allah will not accept his fasting.)"* (Sahih Bukhari)

There are certain things that are required to be abstained from especially during fasting in order to reap maximum benefits, some of which are given as follows:

One of the things to avoid in Ramadan is the excessive desire for flavorsome dishes. The minds of Muslims must not be preoccupied with a variety of foods during Ramadan. There is no need to spend the whole fasting day in preparing myriads of tasty food dishes, as the fast can be broken with simply cooked or naturally available foods. The purpose of fasting is to strengthen our soul by curtailing the desires of our body.

Another thing to avoid in fasting is backbiting. The Qur'an tells us that backbiting is equivalent to eating the flesh of your dead brother (Surah Al-Hujurat: 12). In the hunger of fasting, human flesh tastes very delicious. And it has been observed out of experience that once people engage in gossip, it goes on and on in the form of lying, making fun, slandering, etc., which completely destroys a person's fast. During fasting, people must remember the advice of Umar bin Khattab (may Allah be pleased with him): "Do not talk about people because there is a disease in it; instead, talk about Allah because there is cure in it."

One of the biggest *fitnah* (tribulation) people get trapped in during fasting is to find frivolous ways to kill their time. Some of them watch movies while others view dramas on television or sit in front of Dish TV and keep switching the channels. Still others read novels or spend their time web surfing or chatting on the internet or playing computer games. They do not realize that in the process of killing their time, they also kill the spiritual benefits of fasting.

The best things to do during fasting are to recite the Qur'an and do *tadabbur* (contemplation) on the Qur'an, doing *zikr* (remembrance) of Allah, spending in the path of Allah, etc. Such acts of righteousness during fasting will make us pious (*muttaqun*) which is the whole idea of Islamic fasting.

CHAPTER THREE

Wisdom & Scientific Benefits of Charity (*Zakah* & *Sadaqah*)

ZAKAH (*ZAKAT*) LITERALLY MEANS "PURIFICA-
TION" AND "growth." In the Islamic teachings, *zakah* or
alms-giving is the practice of charitable giving by Muslims
based on accumulated wealth and is obligatory for all who are able to do so.
It is considered a personal responsibility for Muslims to ease economic hard-
ship for others and eliminate inequality. *Zakah* consists of spending a fixed
portion of one's wealth for the benefit of poor or needy, including slaves,
those heavily burdened with paying their debts and travelers who find
themselves in difficult circumstances. A Muslim may also donate more as an
act of voluntary charity (*sadaqah*) in order to achieve additional divine
reward. Why is there so much emphasis on charity and generosity? It is
because charity elevates the human personality by removing selfishness,
greed and materialism. It creates compassion, care, love, and kindness. It
makes a person more thankful to Allah. It helps those who are in need, and
it provides funds for good causes and for community projects.

   Zakah is one of the five pillars of Islam. The other four are a declaration of faith in one God and in Prophet Muhammad, the five daily
prayers, fasting the month of Ramadan and once-in-a-lifetime pilgrimage
(*Hajj*) to Makkah (which is an obligation for those who have the physical and financial ability to undertake the journey). In the Qur'an, there
are five words used for charity: *zakah* (obligatory charity), *sadaqah*
(voluntary charity), *khairaat* (good deeds), *ihsan* (kindness and consider-
ation), *infaq fi Sabil Allah* (spending in the path of Allah). This spending
could be disclosed, or it could be done secretly. The Qur'an tells us: *"If
you disclose the act of charity, it is well, but if you conceal it and give it to the
poor, that is better for you. (Allah) will forgive you some of your sins. And*

Allah is Well-Acquainted with what you do." (Surah Al-Baqarah: 271) According to Imam At-Tabari and other Islamic scholars, there is scholarly consensus (ijmaa) to give *zakah* openly while giving *sadaqah* secretly to people. (Fathul Baari: Vol 6, pg 22) It is an obligation on Muslims to pay 1/40th (2.5%) of the wealth which they have had for a full lunar year, 2.5% of goods used for trade, and 5% or 10% of certain type of harvests depending on irrigation. Exempt from *zakah* are a person's house and personal transportation.

Zakah is not to be taken as an economic due because its main purpose, as the term implies, is to spiritually purify the person who is giving the *zakah*. It is mentioned in the Qur'an:

> *"Take alms (zakah and sadaqah) from their wealth in order to purify them and sanctify them with it."* (Surah At-Tawbah: 103)

Similarly, the Qur'an tells us:

> *"By no means shall you attain righteousness until you spend (in the way of Allah) out of that which you cherish most, and whatever you spend, Allah is aware of it."* (Surah Ale-Imran: 92)

This chapter is not meant to describe the juristic aspects of *zakah* or *sadaqah*, types of wealth on which to pay *zakah*, how to distribute it, etc. Such details can be found in any book of Islamic fiqh (jurisprudence). Instead, the main focus here is to describe the wisdom and scientific benefits of paying *zakah* and *sadaqah* because when we spend in the path of Allah, its ultimate benefit comes to us as mentioned in the Qur'an:

> *"And whatever you spend in good, it is for your own benefit, when you spend not except seeking Allah's Countenance. And whatever you spend in good, it will be repaid to you in full, and you shall not be wronged."* (Surah Al-Baqarah: 272)

RELATIONSHIP OF *SALAH* & *ZAKAH* (PRAYERS AND CHARITY)

When we read the Qur'an, we notice that *salah* and *zakah* almost always appear together in the Qur'an. For example:

32

"And perform salah and give zakah, and lend to Allah a goodly loan." (Surah Muzzammil: 20)

"Truly those who believe, and do deeds of righteousness, and perform salah, and give zakah, they will have their reward with their Lord. On them shall be no fear, nor shall they grieve." (Surah Al-Baqarah: 277)

In fact, *salah* and *zakah* are mentioned together in the Qur'an twenty-eight times. Abdullah ibn Mas'ud, a well-known companion of the Prophet (peace be upon him), gave the verdict: *"The one who denies paying zakah is no longer a Muslim and such person's salah is also not accepted."*[32] The first caliph, Abu Bakr Siddique, clearly saw the link between *salah* and *zakah* when he ruled that those people who refused to pay *zakah* are leaving Islam, and he fought them because of that, and he used to say: *"By Allah, I will certainly fight anyone who separates zakah from salah."* (Bukhari, Muslim, Abu Dawud, Ahmed, Nisa'ee)

Salah is a sign of our love for Allah and *zakah* is an indication of our love for His people. Just like prayers represent our relationship to Allah, in the same way, spending in the path of Allah represents our relationship to His creatures. Dr. Ali Shariati noted in his book *On the Sociology of Islam* that the Qur'an begins with the word "Allah" (Bismillah Ar-Rehman Ar-Raheem – In the name of Allah, the Most Beneficent, the Most Merciful (Surah Al-Fatiha: 1) and it ends with the word "An-Naas" (People). Hence, the Qur'an is a link between Allah and His people.[33] By the same token, it can be said that *salah* shows our link with the Creator while *zakah* (and *sadaqah*) is a manifestation of our link with His creation. In this context, it can be easily understood why giving alms and charity to people has been equated with lending money to Allah. *"If you give Allah a goodly loan,' He will increase it for you several fold and will forgive you."* (Surah At-Taghabun: 17) After all, the

---

[32] Fiqh al-Maluk (vol.1); Ibn Abi Sheeba (vol.1); Kitabul Khiraaj Abi Yusuf quoted in: Qal'a Jee, Dr. Mohammad Rawwas (Az Zahran University, Saudi Arabia) (1992). *Fiqh Abdullah bin Mas'ud.* Lahore, Idara Ma'arif Islami.

[33] Shariati, Dr. Ali (1979). *On the Sociology of Islam.* Berkeley (California), Mizan Press.

ultimate goal in spending on the needy and the poor is to seek the pleasure of Allah.

Great Bosnian intellectual Alija Izetbegovic elucidates the link between *salah* and *zakah* in the following words:

> "In that focus, *salah* is seen as a spiritual and *zakah* as a social component. *Salah* is directed toward man and *zakah* toward the world; *salah* has a personal and *zakah* a social character; *salah* is an instrument of upbringing and *zakah* a component of social order. Almost all Islamic thinkers agree on a certain type of dependence between *salah* as a personal prayer and *zakah* as a social attitude in harmony with *salah*. This opinion even led to the conclusion that *salah*, if not strictly followed *by zakah, has no use.*"[34]

Izetbegovic further states that the relationship of *salah* and *zakah* is similar to the more general relationship of having faith and doing good deeds (Imaan and Amal saalih). In light of this relationship, *salah* and *zakah* can be considered as the two pillars upon which the whole building of Islam rests. An important verse of the Qur'an which shows the relationship of faith and good deeds with *salah* and *zakah* is where Allah says:

> *"As to those who believe and do good deeds, establish the salah and pay the Zakah, they will most surely have their reward with their Lord and they will have nothing to fear nor to grieve."* (Surah Al-Baqarah: 277)

RELATIONSHIP OF *SADAQAH* & *TAQWAH* (CHARITY AND GOD-CONSCIOUSNESS)

In the Qur'an, the word "*taqwa*" (God-consciousness) has almost always appeared along with "*Infaaq fi sabeel illah*" (spending for the sake of Allah). This means that God-consciousness and purification of the

---

[34] Izetbegovic, 'Alija 'Ali (1994). *Islam Between East and West*. Indiana, American Trust Publications.

heart cannot be achieved without spending for the sake of Allah as the Qur'an asserts: *"So he who gives (in charity) and fears Allah (becomes God-conscious)."* (Surah Al-Lail: 5-10)

In Qur'an, we will also notice that whenever the subject of spending in the path of Allah (*Infaaq*) is mentioned, its opposite, i.e., either subject of interest (*Ribaa*; usury) or miserliness (*bukhal*) is mentioned along with it. By contrasting it with its opposites, the concept of infaaq is made even clearer. In Arabic there is a saying that translates as follows:

"Things are recognized by their opposites."

Hence, by mentioning its opposite, the concept of giving for the sake of Allah has been accentuated. Similarly, in the Qur'an in Surah Al-Imran, when God-conscious people are mentioned, their qualities are also talked about:

"Those who show patience, firmness and self-control; who are true (in word and deed); who worship devoutly; who spend (in the way of Allah); and who pray for forgiveness in the early hours of the morning." (Surah Al-Imran: 17)

Keeping in view the concept of coherence (nazm) in the Qur'an, there is a subtle point in the sequence of the list mentioned in this verse of the Qur'an. Since the quality of spending in the way of Allah has been mentioned before the attribute of praying and seeking forgiveness in the early hours of dawn, the later can only be achieved if one spends in the way of Allah.

Piety and God-consciousness (taqwa) are feelings which exist deep in our hearts. It has been mentioned in a tradition of Prophet Muhammad (peace be upon him) that the best of alms is that, which the right hand gives and the left hand knows not of. The Prophet (peace be upon him) said: *"Seven people will be shaded by Allah under His shade on the day (of Judgment) when there will be no shade except of His throne. One of them will be a person who practices charity so secretly that his left hand does not know what his right hand has given."* (Bukhari - *Kitab Az-Zakah*) This *hadeeth* means that a person should give *zakah* and charity in such a way that people do not know about it. The purpose of this commandment is to instill sincerity in the hearts of Muslims. The only goal of a person giving charity secretly is to please Allah. Such a person expects appreciation and reward only from Allah. That is the whole spirit of piety or God-consciousness (*taqwa*) in Islam.

MEDICAL BENEFITS OF GIVING ZAKAH & SADAQAH

Prophet Muhammad (peace be upon him) said in a tradition narrated by Abu Huraira:

> *"I heard Allah's Apostle saying, 'Whoever is pleased that he be granted more wealth and that his lease of life be pro longed, then he should keep good relations with his Kith and kin.' "* (Sahih Bukhari – Kitab Al-Adab)

In another *hadeeth*, Prophet Muhammad (peace be upon him) said:

> *"Charity cools the wrath of Allah and safeguards the giver against a disgraceful death."* (Tirmidhi)

In one *hadeeth* narrated by Thawban, the Prophet (peace be upon him) said:

> *"Only supplication can ward off predestination, and only righteousness prolongs a life span."* (Ibn Habban)

Modern medical science has started to understand some of the wisdoms behind the sayings of Prophet Muhammad (peace be upon him) 1400 years after they were uttered. From the years 1967 to 1969, social scientists House, Robbins and Metzner conducted a study on the residents of Tecumseh, a city in the state of Michigan.[35] In this study published in the 1982 issue of the *American Journal of Epidemiology*, medical examinations (e.g., blood tests) and interviews were conducted in

---

[35] House, J.S., Robbins C., & Metzner H. (1982) The association of social relationships and activities with mortality: Prospective evidence from the Tecumseh Community Health Study. *American Journal of Epidemiology* 116:123-140.

1967-1969 with mortality over the succeeding 9 to 12 years on a group of 2,754 adult (aged 35–69 years as of 1967–1969) men and women. It was found in the results of the study that people who had a higher level of social relationships and activities were significantly less likely to die during the follow-up period. In other words, people who are more active and more beneficial to the society are the ones who live longer compared to those people who do not have such attributes.

When a person benefits less-fortunate people of the society by giving them *zakah* and charity, he/she not only gets spiritual peace but also his/her heart becomes filled with the feelings of compassion and care, which in itself has beneficial and long-lasting effects on the body. Rollin McCraty and his associates have shown in laboratory experiments at the HeartMath Institute (Boulder Creek, CA) that when the subjects of an experiment focus on their hearts and activate a core heart feeling such as love, care or appreciation, such a focus changes their heart rhythms immediately. When positive emotions such as happiness, compassion, care, and appreciation are activated, they result in decreased production of the stress hormone 'cortisol' which speeds up the aging process in our body. Instead, positive emotions result in increasing DHEA production in the body, a hormone that fights aging in our body.[36]

In the same vein, a more interesting research comes from Glen Rein, PhD, Mike Atkinson and Rollin McCraty published in the 1995 summer issue of the *Journal of Advancement in Medicine*.[37] This study was conducted on a total of 30 subjects in which 13 were males and 17 were females. They were all in good health and were free from any infection or disease. They all shared the same work schedule, sleep cycle and diet

---

[36] McCraty, R., B. Barrios-Choplin , D. Rozman , M. Atkinson , A. Watkins. (1998) "The impact of a new emotional self-management program on stress, emotions, heart rate variability, DHEA and cortisol." *Integrative Physiological and Behavioral Science* 33(2): 151-170.

[37] Rein, Glen, Mike Atkinson and Rollin McCraty (Summer 1995). "The Physiological and Psychological Effects of Compassion and Anger." *Journal of Advancement in Medicine* 8(2).

habits. They all refrained from smoking, exercising, or drinking anything except water. Feelings of care and compassion were induced by two different methods: Intentionally self-inducing the feelings and externally stimulating them with video tapes. In the self-induction method, the participants were asked to focus on feelings of care or compassion toward someone or something. In the external method of inducing positive emotions, participants were asked to freely experience all emotions felt when watching a video tape of Mother Teresa, a Roman Catholic nun caring for the diseased and dying in the slums of Calcutta, a city of India. Negative emotional states were induced by self-recall and video stimulation methods. Self-induced emotions were accomplished by asking subjects to recall situations in their own lives which arouse feelings of anger or frustration. Subjects were asked to recall and maintain their negative feelings as best they could. In the second method, participants were instructed to experience all emotions aroused while watching a specially edited video of war scenes.

One of the main findings of this study was that a 5 minute period of experiencing care and compassion immediately produced a significant increase in S-IgA (secretory IgA) levels, while anger and frustration did not. After watching the video of Mother Teresa, test subjects had an increase of 17 percent in S-IgA levels. S-IgA (secretory IgA) is a type of antibody present in our saliva and throughout our bodies and it is our first line of defense against invading bacteria and viruses. Hence, S-IgA levels are an important measurement of the health of our immune (defense) system.

More important than that, it was observed in those experiments that after five minutes of self-induced feelings of care and compassion, the subjects had an immediate 41 percent average increase in their S-IgA levels. After one hour, their S-IgA levels returned to normal, but then slowly increased over the next six hours. Thus, self-induced care actually resulted in a larger rise in S-IgA than the indirect feeling of care evoked by the Mother Teresa video. Researchers also observed that when the participants experienced anger, their heart rate increased and their S-IgA levels had dropped to 50 % of normal levels and even after 6 hours, their S-IgA levels were still not back to normal.

This research demonstrates that negative feelings such as anger and stinginess (which is a form of negative feeling due to its pessimism) can impair our body's defense system. Conversely, feelings of care and compassion produce a significant increase in our defense system, which may last up to 6 hours. Hence, nurturing in ourselves the feelings of positive emotions of care and compassion for other members of our society enhances the defense system of our body, which, as a consequence, increases our life span.

These findings also suggest that if our body's defense system gets a boost just by imagining to help the poor and needy people, what would be the effect on our bodies of actually financially helping the poor people in our real life. Such genuine feelings will surely result in increasing our life span. Indeed, giving for God's sake is healthy for us and healthy for the society we live in. Doc Childre of The HeartMath Institute notes in his book, *The HeartMath Solution* that many scientific researches show that when a person is cared for and he cares for other people and shows compassion towards them, this plays a far more important role in improving one's health and expanding life span compared to controlling factors such as blood pressure, cholesterol or smoking, etc. [38]

LEFT BRAIN VERSUS RIGHT BRAIN AND GIVING THE CHARITY

Based on the current findings in the field of anatomy and biopsychology, the human brain is divided into two halves: left and right hemispheres. The two of them are separated by a thin membrane called corpus callosum. The left and the right hemispheres of the brain perform different functions. The left brain uses logic, excels in math and science, deals with words and language, is detail oriented, and it tries to play safe. The right brain, on the other hand, uses logic, is inclined to philosophy and religion, is "big picture" oriented, has the capacity to believe (have faith), is imaginative, and is risk taking.

---

[38] Childre, Doc & Martin, Howard (1999). *The HeartMath Solution*. New York, HarperSanFrancisco.

As we know our whole life on this planet is a struggle between opposite forces – our spiritual being versus our material being. This struggle always manifests itself when we attempt to perform spiritually-invigorating deeds. The human brain comprising of left and right hemispheres is no exception in this struggle. When we give *zakah* and *sadaqah* under the influence of "right brain", our "left brain" opposes this decision. As stated above, the right brain is risk taking despite the fear of getting poor after spending on the needy people. The right brain is capable of holistic thinking, able to "believe" (have Imaan) that when we spend in the way of Allah, we are given more in this world as well as in the Life Hereafter. Because of the imaginative powers of right brain, a person can visualize the rewards of the paradise. On the other hand, since the left brain thinks logically, it becomes engaged in counting as noted in the Qur'an: *"He who has gathered wealth and counted it."* (Surah Al-Humazah: 2) The left brain makes the person think that he has earned this wealth with so much hard work, why should he spend this wealth on the poor people. It is this counting nature of the left brain about which psychologist Mihaly Csikszentmihalyi talked about in his book *The Evolving Self* when he mentioned that our brain is inclined more towards pessimism and always expects the worse to happen. It does not fall completely asleep because it is "mortality phobic." In this way, the human brain remains ready for the unexpected.[39] It is this fear and pessimism of the left brain that is exploited by Satan (devil) when we want to spend in the path of Allah: *"Satan threatens you with poverty."* (Surah Al-Baqarah: 268) Hence, Satan takes full advantage of the hidden fears of the left brain.

The attitude of the left brain is more of a selfish kind, which is only concerned about its own survival whereas the outlook of the right brain is more of the humanistic type, which cares about other people as well. American scientist Paul Pearsall writes in his book *The Heart's Code* that the brain's left hemisphere tends to be more "hard and coldly logical" while the right brain more "softly emotional" and our present materialistic world tends to be more left brain-dominated.[40] In this materialistic

---

[39] Csikszentmihalyi, Mihaly (1993). *The Evolving Self.* New York, Harper Collins.
[40] Pearsall, Paul Ph.D. (1998). *The Heart's Code.* New York, Broadway Books.

world, we need to care for people and practice charity by utilizing more of our right brain.

EASE IN THE VIRTUOUS ACTS BY GIVING *ZAKAH* & *SADAQAH*

One benefit of spending in the path of Allah is that it becomes easy for the person giving charity to perform righteous deeds; otherwise, the rule in this world is that the path of righteousness is hard whereas the path to sin is easy. For this reason, we find fewer people on the path of righteousness as Prophet Jesus (peace be upon him) said in a saying attributed to him:

"But small is the gate and narrow the road that leads to life, and few are there that find it." (Mathew 7:14)

In fact, the term used in the Qur'an for the levels of Paradise is "dara-jaat" (meaning, the ascending steps) because it is hard to go up on a stairway. We are going against the gravity. We are going against our carnal desires. Conversely, the Quranic term for the levels in the Hell is "darakaat" (descending steps) because it is easy to go down. No effort is exerted as we are going in the direction of the gravity. However, charity is such an act that Allah makes ascension on the stairway towards the Paradise easy for that person. This topic has been touched upon in Surah Al-Balad in the Qur'an:

"And did We (Allah) not show him (human being) the two high-roads (of good and evil)? But he has made no effort to pass on the path that is steep. And what do you know what that difficult steep is? It is freeing someone's neck from slavery; or giving food on a day of hunger to an orphan near of kin; or to a destitute lying in dust." (Surah Al-Balad: 10-16)

These verses of the Qur'an mean that one of the two paths shown to man by God leads to heights but it is toilsome and steep; man has to tread it against the desires of his self and the temptations of Satan. The other path is easy which descends down, but does not require any toil from man; one only needs to give free reins to one's desires, and, consequently, one automatically goes on rolling down the abyss. The benefit of spending for the sake of God is that it becomes easier for us to perform acts of virtue since our hearts become pure of the diseases of love of wealth and miserliness. In Qur'an, Allah says:

"So he who gives (in charity) and fears (Allah), And (in all sincerity) testifies to the best, We will indeed make smooth for him the path to Bliss. But he who is a greedy miser and thinks himself self-sufficient, And rejects the best, We will indeed make smooth for him the path to Misery." (Surah Al-Lail: 5-10)

INCREASE IN WISDOM BY GIVING *ZAKAH* & *SADAQAH*

Another benefit of spending in the path of Allah is that Allah grants wisdom to those who spend in His path as mentioned in the Qur'an:

"Shaitaan (Satan) threatens you with poverty and orders you to commit Fahshaa (evil deeds, lewdness, etc.); whereas Allah promises you Forgiveness from Himself and Bounty, and Allah is All-Sufficient for His creatures' needs, All-Knower. He grants wisdom to whom He pleases, and he, to whom wisdom is granted, is indeed granted abundant good...." (Surah Al-Baqarah: 268-269)

When a person gives charity, Allah grants him wisdom and the person's heart becomes deep rooted in faith. He is granted steadfastness in the path of righteousness. He is granted the correct understanding and knowledge of religion because God is pleased with him. In one tradition narrated by Muawiya, Prophet Muhammad (peace be upon him) said: *"If Allah wants to do good to a person, He makes him comprehend the religion."* (Sahih Bukhari)

INCREASE IN WEALTH BY GIVING *ZAKAH* & *SADAQAH*

Another advantage of spending on the poor and needy is the increase in wealth as it has been promised by Allah in the Qur'an in the following words:

"Allah will destroy Ribaa (usury; interest) and will give increase for Sadaqaat (deeds of charity, alms, etc.)." (Surah Al-Baqarah: 276)

Not only is the person giving charity rewarded in the life of Hereafter but also his/her wealth increases in this world. One of the reasons for the increase in wealth of the person giving charity is the supplications to Allah of those poor and needy people who are benefiting from that charity. Those people who raise their hands in supplication are the ones who are destitute and broken-hearted – people who deserve that their prayers be answered by their Lord owing to their state of poverty and privation. Prophet Muhammad (peace be upon him) said in a tradition:

"You are given help and provision because of your weak ones." (Al-Bukhari)

This tells us that when we help the indigent and poor people, Allah causes an increase in our wealth because of the invocations of those people. Some of the Prophetic traditions inform us that even the angels supplicate for the increase in the wealth of a person who helps the poor and resource less people of the society as mentioned in one of the *hadeeth*:

Every morning when a person gets up, two Angels come down. One of them says: "Oh Allah, give the charitable person success." The other Angel says: "Oh Allah, bring destruction upon the miser." (Sahih Bukhari; Sahih Muslim)

The Qur'an repeatedly advises us not to be stingy and treat the needy and poor with love and respect: *"Have you seen him who denies the Recompense? That is he who repulses the orphan (harshly), And urges not the feeding of the poor."* (Surah Al-Ma'un) And in another place, the Qur'an advises: *"Therefore, treat not the orphan with oppression. And repulse not the beggar."* (Surah Ad-Duha: 9, 10) In this context, it is interesting to note the story of a man and the beggar quoted by Abdul-Malik Mujahid in his book *Gems and Jewels* (In Arabic: Al-Lulu al-Manthur):

"A story has been related about a man who once sat with his wife to eat a barbecued chicken. A beggar then knocked on the door, and when the man went to answer it, he scolded the beggar and drove him away. It was the will of Allah that afterwards that same man should become poor and should be bereft of all material possessions; because of his poverty, he had to divorce his wife. She married another man, and one day she was sitting with him to eat a barbecued chicken, when someone knocked on the door. The man said to his wife, 'Give this chicken to the man at the door.' When she opened it, she was shocked to realize that it was her first husband. She gave him the chicken and returned, crying. Her husband asked her what was the matter, and she informed him that the man at the door was her previous husband. She then told him about the story of the beggar that her previous husband had scolded and sent away, and her husband said, 'By Allah, I was that beggar.'"[41]

AVOIDING THE THINGS WHICH POLLUTE *ZAKAH* & *SADAQAH*

The biggest obstacle in giving *zakah* and *sadaqah* is stinginess. It is mentioned in a Prophetic tradition: *"Be aware of stinginess. It destroyed many nations before you. It made them to shed the blood of each other and misappropriate what was sacrosanct."* (Sahih Muslim)

Imam Abu Hamid Al-Ghazali in his magnum opus book *Ihya Uloom ad-Deen* (The Revival of the Religious Sciences) states that the best cure for the disease of stinginess is that the person should continuously spend for the sake of Allah. In this way, this disease will weaken over time. In addition, when a person gives larger amount in charity for the sake of Allah, on the psychological level now it becomes easier for such person to spend smaller amount in charity. Once someone asked Sheikh Ashraf Ali Thanawi as to how would he know if his charity has been accepted in the sight of his Lord? Sheikh Thanawi replied that when we give charity in an amount that we feel some pain in our self, then that means our charity is accepted.

---

[41] Mujahid, Abdul-Malik (2004). *Gems and Jewels*. Riyadh, Saudi Arabia, Darussalam Publishers.

Other things that are needed to be abstained from when giving charity are given as follows: A person must never remind those whom he had helped about his favors on the latter and must never repulse the beggar harshly as mentioned in the Qur'an: *"Therefore, treat not the orphan with oppression. And repulse not the beggar."* (Surah Ad-Duha: 9, 10) Moreover, a person giving charity should not have any desire to show off and seek praise from others. It takes away sincerity and seriousness from the act of virtue a person is performing and his actions become superficial. It is important to remember that any deeds carried out with the intention of being seen by others will not incur any reward. The same applies to giving *sadaqah*. Furthermore, the person giving charity should not feel himself in any way superior to the one being given the charity because arrogance is a deadly disease of the heart. In this respect, the advice of Imam Ibn Qayyim is worth remembering that a person giving charity ought to be thankful to the poor and needy accepting the charity for it is due to that indigent and poor person that the former has been able to earn the reward of giving charity. [42]

Zakah and *sadaqah* have to be from lawfully earned money. There is no room for Robin Hood-like acts in Islam. Money from interest or gambling or pornography or credit card purchases with the intention of not paying back is absolutely unacceptable in Islam, let alone it be given as a charity. When giving *zakah* and *sadaqah*, a man's poor relatives, orphans, widows, etc. have to first right to get that help. According to one *hadeeth*, there is a double reward for the charity given to a poor relative – one for giving the charity itself and the other for binding the family ties. Indeed, charity begins at home. Last, but certainly not the least, the following words of the Prophet Muhammad (peace be upon him) are worth remembering:

"Stinginess and Imaan (faith) can never be together in the heart of a believing servant."(Sahih Bukhari, Sunan An-Nisa'i, Musnad Ahmad, Al-Hakim)

---

[42] Ibn Al-Qayyem, al-Jawziyyah (2004). *Al-Fawaid: A Collection of Wise Sayings.* AL-Mansura, Egypt, Umm Al-Qura. (Rendered into English by Bayan Translation Services)

HUMAN BEINGS CREATED FOR SHARING & CARING

In addition to the rights of their Creator over them, the human beings also have certain rights of their fellow society members over them. As human beings, we must give and take for God's sake. Dr. Mohammad Iqbal, the famous Islamic poet and philosopher said in one of his poems:

"Man is created to feel the needs of other human beings,
Otherwise, angels were more than sufficient to God for worship."
(Bang-e-Dara) [43]

Islam teaches us that those who are always mindful of the weak and the poor and constantly strive for their welfare are engaged in perpetual worship. Abu Hurairah reported that the Prophet (peace be upon him) said: *"One who strives to help the widows and the poor is like the one who fights in the way of Allah."* The narrator said: I think that he (peace be upon him) added also: *"I shall regard him as the one who stands up (for prayer) without rest and as the one who observes fasts continuously."* (Bukhari and Muslim)

In the early years of Islam while Muslims were in Makkah, the paying of *zakah* was voluntary. However, once the Islamic state was established in Madinah by Prophet Muhammad (peace be upon him), *zakah* was made obligatory by Allah. For this reason, *zakah* has been mentioned only 8 times in the Surahs (chapters) of the Qur'an revealed in Makkah but it is mentioned 22 times in the Surahs revealed in Madinah. Islam understands that poverty is the mother of many social evils. Ever since the Muslim countries of the present times have stopped the implementation of the *zakah* system, the financial conditions of Muslims have become worse. However, many Muslims still carry out this duty at the individual levels. This is the reason that any non-Muslim visitor to a Muslim country notices mercy, care and compassion in every Muslim society even in this age of materialism. Sharing and caring are the hallmark of any Muslim society because Islam teaches the members of a Muslim society to be an embodiment

---

[43] Iqbal, Sir Mohammad (Allama) (1987). *Bang-e-Dara*. Lahore, Sheikh Ghulam Ali & Sons.

of Allah's Messenger (peace be upon him) who has been described as: *"O Muhammad, We have sent you to be a real blessing for the people of the world."* (Surah Al-Anbiya: 107). The highest moral quality which Prophet Muhammad (peace be upon him) tried to inculcate among his followers was this very quality of mercy and care. Consider, for example, the following of his sayings, which shows what importance he attached to it:

• Jarir bin Abdullah narrates that the Holy Prophet (peace be upon him) said: *"Allah does not show mercy to him who does not show mercy to others."* (Bukhari, Muslim)

• Abdullah bin Amr bin al-Aas says that the Prophet (peace be upon him) said: *"The Rahman (Merciful) shows mercy to those who show mercy (to others). Show mercy to those who live in the earth, the One who is in heaven will show mercy to you."* (Abu Da'ud, Tirmidhi)

• In a tradition narrated by Iyad bin Humad, Prophet Muhammad (peace be upon him) said: *"Three kinds of men belong to Paradise, one of whom is the person who is kindly and compassionate to every relative and every Muslim."* (Muslim)

• Nu'man bin Bashir has reported that the Holy Prophet said: *"You will find the believers like a body in the matter of mutual kindness, love and sympathy, so that if one part of the body suffers the whole body suffers and becomes restless because of it."* (Bukhari, Muslim)

• Abdullah bin Umar has reported that the Holy Prophet (peace be upon him) said: *"A Muslim is a brother of the other Muslim: neither treats him unjustly, nor withholds his help from him. The person who works to fulfill a need of his brother, Allah will seek to fulfill his need; and the one who rescues a Muslim from an affliction, Allah will rescue him from an affliction of the afflictions of the Resurrection Day; and the one who conceals the fault of a Muslim, Allah will conceal his fault on the Resurrection Day."* (Bukhari, Muslim)

• *"The generous person is near Allah, near Paradise & near the people and the miser is far from Paradise, far from the people and near Hell. And the illiterate charitable man is dearer to Allah than the pious miser."* (Tirmidhi)

• *"A Muslim who plants a tree or sows a field, from which man, birds and animals can eat, is committing an act of charity."* (Muslim)

• *"What actions are most excellent? To gladden the heart of human beings, to feed the hungry, to help the afflicted, to lighten the sorrow of the sorrowful, and to remove the sufferings of the injured."* (Bukhari)

• *"The worst food is the food of the marriage banquet to which the rich are invited and from which the poor are left out."* (Muslim)

These traditions indicate the kind of a society as envisioned by the Quranic instruction Islamic teachings – a society where people give and take for God's sake.

LEARNING LESSONS FROM OTHERS

The greatest embodiment of generosity for mankind is Prophet Muhammad (peace be upon him) although every prophet of Allah is an example of generosity to be followed. Ibn Abbas (may Allah be pleased with him), the cousin of Prophet Muhammad (peace be upon him), said: *"The Prophet of Allah was the most generous of people, and he was even more generous during Ramadan when Angle Jibreel (archangel Gabriel) met him. Gabriel used to meet him every night in Ramadan until it was over and the Prophet would go through the Qur'an with him. The Messenger of Allah was more generous with good things than the blowing wind (which brings rain and welfare)."* (Bukhari)

When the first revelation came to Prophet Muhammad (peace be upon him) while he was contemplating in the cave of mount Hira, wide-awake and fully conscious, Angle Jibreel appeared to him and brought the first five verses of Surah Al-Alaq from the Qur'an: "Read (O Muhammad) in the name of thy Lord; Who created man from a clot. Read: and thy Lord is the Most Bounteous. Who taught by the pen, Taught man that which he knew not." Dizzy and frightened by the strange experience which had never occurred to him earlier, the Messenger of Allah (peace be upon him) came back with verses, his heart trembling, and went to Khadijah (may Allah be pleased with her) and said: *"Wrap me up, wrap me up!"* for he still felt horrified himself. Khadijah (May Allah be pleased with her) asked the reason for the Prophet's

48

(peace be upon him) restlessness and the latter told her what had happened. Khadijah was intelligent and prudent. She was the wife of the Prophet (peace be upon him). She had spent many years with him as the closest companion and knew him like she knew herself. She knew in her heart that the good grace of God could never allow one so high-minded, truth-loving, trustworthy and upright man such as her husband, to be possessed by a jinn or a devil. She knew that God would never abandon a person like Prophet Muhammad (peace be upon him) who was always the first and foremost when it came to helping the poor and indigent, caring for the widows and loving the orphans. And so she assured him with domineering self-confidence: By no means; I swear to God that He would never embarrass you. Because you consolidate and salvage relationships, you speak the truth, you bear peoples burdens, you help the destitute, you entertain guests and you relieved the pain and grief suffered for the sake of truth. (*Mishkat al-Masabih,* Vol. IV, p. 1253)

The Messenger of Allah (peace be upon him) never turned anyone down if he could afford helping him. It was narrated that a man asked the Messenger of Allah to give him a new garment he had on him. With absolutely no hesitation, he gave his garment to the one seeking it. (Tirmidhi) Jabir (may Allah be pleased with him) reported: *"Messenger of Allah (peace be upon him) never said 'no' to anyone who asked him for anything."* (Bukhari & Muslim)

This trait of generosity has become the model for his companions as well. On the expedition of Tabuk when Muslims had a shortage of funds, the Prophet (peace be upon him) made a general call to all his companions for financial help. On that occasion, Umar Al-Farooq brought half of his wealth for donation. Uthman bin Afaan supplied forty thousand gold coins for the expedition of Tabuk and, in addition to that, he would donate all his business caravans for the sake of Allah during the time of need and famine. On the occasion of Tabuk, the closest of all the companions to Prophet Muhammad (peace be upon him), Abu Bakr (may Allah be pleased with him) arrived a little late. When he was asked for the reason of his late coming, Abu Bakr's response amazed everyone. Abu Bakr told the Prophet (peace be upon him) that he was trying to make sure that there is not a needle left in his home and he donated all his wealth for the sake of Allah. When the Messenger (peace be upon him) asked him as to what did he leave for his family, Abu Bakr replied: *"I have left the name of Allah and His Messenger (peace be upon him) for my family."* Ayesha (may Allah be pleased with her), who grew up in the house of the two most generous of all, her husband the messenger of Allah and her father Abu Bakr, gave away more than a hundred thousand dirham while she was fasting. When her servant told her she could have left something for their Iftaar (breaking of the fast), she said: *"If you had reminded me earlier, I could have done that."* Despite her poverty, Ayesha forgot her own house when she was giving charity to the poor. Such are the examples of all the companions of the Prophet (peace be upon him). [44/45]

Islamic history is filled with the glittering examples of those who surpassed everyone in giving charity and caring for their fellow members of the society. One of those glittering examples is that of Imam Ibn Taymiyyah. He was a very distinguished and famous Muslim scholar in both rational and religious sciences. He was an expert in the Quranic sciences and Fiqh (Islamic jurisprudence). He was persecuted and imprisoned several times for some of his verdicts, and eventually died in prison in 728 Hijra. At one time, Ibn Taymiyyah was thrown into prison because of a legal ruling he gave about the issue of divorce. Later, he recalled that incident and wrote in his *Majmoo'ul Fataawa*: "I would provide for some families before I was put in prison, and when I was imprisoned, this aide was cut off to these poor families. So, I was extremely pained by this, and the news would come to me from these families while I was in prison: "You still come to us in the same physical form, and you pay us the same amount that you used to give us." So, our brothers from the jinn are stepping up to take over from what we used to do. If the Earth is empty of anyone to do good, the world of the believing jinn and angels are with the believer." [46]

[44] Lings, Martin (1983). *Muhammad: His Life Based on the Earliest Sources*. London, U.K., The Islamic Texts Society.
[45] Tabari, Mohammad Ibn Jareer (1987). *Taarikh Umamm wal Mulook*. Karachi, Nafees Academy.
[46] Ibn Taymiyyah, Taiq ud Din Ahmed (1381 Hijra) *Majmoo'ul Fataawa Sheikh ul Islam*. Riyadh, Ma'taabe Ar-Riyadh.

The exemplary spirit of generosity of the companions of Prophet Muhammad (peace be upon him) was embodied in the Arab merchants who went to Southeast Asia (including India) and Far East Asia (including Indonesia and Malaysia). People of those places were so much impressed by the generosity of the Muslim merchants that they accepted Islam. Today, the same spirit of generosity still permeates the Bedouins in the villages and deserts of every part of the Middle East. Mohammad Asad (formerly Leopold Weiss – an Austrian Jewish convert to Islam) writes in his famous book *The Road to Mecca* that when he was a journalist and he started his travel in the Middle East, their train was crossing the Sinai desert. There was a Bedouin sitting close to him. Asad continues:

"The bedouin opposite me rose slowly, unwound his headcloth and opened the window. His face was thin, brown, sharply drawn, one of those hawk faces which always look intently ahead. He bought a piece of cake, turned around and was about to sit down, when his eye fell on me; and, without a word, he broke his cake in two and offered me half. When he saw my hesitation and astonishment, he smiled – and I saw that the tender smile fitted his face as well as the intentness of a moment ago – and said a word which I could not understand then but now known was tafaddal – 'grant me the favour.' I took the cake and thanked him with a nod. Another traveler – he wore, with the exception of his red fez, European clothes and may have been a small trader – intervened as translator. In halting English he said:

'He say, you traveler, he traveler; your way and his way is together.'

When I now think of this little occurrence, it seems to me that all my later love for the Arab character must have been influenced by it. For in the gesture of this bedouin, who, over all barriers of strangeness, sensed a friend in an accidental traveling companion and broke bread with him, I must already have felt the breath and the step of a humanity free of burden."[47]

---

[47] Asad, Muhammad (2002). *The Road to Mecca.* Malaysia, Islamic Book Trust.

The truth of the matter is that Allah does not waste the reward of anyone who performs any act of charity, whether Muslim or non-Muslim, provided that there is sincerity in it and it is done not for showing off but for the sake of God only. For brevity's sake, just one example of Einstein's parents is given here. Albert Einstein (1879 – 1955) is regarded as the father of modern physics. Yet there was a time during his school years when his teachers in Germany told him that he would never amount to anything because his questions destroyed classroom discipline. One of the teachers told Einstein's mother that he was a "lazy dog." Discouraged by his school teachers' attitudes, Einstein dropped out of school. However, one day Einstein's parents invited a poor and impoverished student named Max Talmey to dinner "in an act of charity and compassion."[48] Max brought a book of popular science and gave it as a gift to Einstein. Later on in his life, Einstein recalled that his latent interest in science was awakened by that popular science book given to him by that poor student. In fact, the first page of Bernstein's *People's Book of Natural Science* described the astonishing speed of electricity through wires and light through space. Einstein began to wonder what it would be like to travel at the speed of light. Eventually, Einstein propounded his famous theory of relativity about the light which marked the beginning of modern physics. Hence, a small act of charity by Einstein's parents changed the life of their son. No doubt as the Qur'an says: "Can the reward of goodness be any other than goodness? Then, which of the favors of your Lord will you (men and jinn) – deny? (Surah Ar-Rahman: 60, 61)

IN A NUTSHELL

Examples of spending for the sake of Allah include feeding the poor people, financial help of our poor relatives, orphans, widows as well as other less fortunate people, supporting the building of mosques, hospitals and Islamic educational institutions, helping someone to establish himself in business, helping someone to recover from some disease by monetary assistance, all such charitable works come under *sadaqah*. The scope of

[48] Sagan, Carl (1980). *Cosmos*. New York, Random House.

sadaqah is so vast that even the poor who may have nothing can offer some form of *sadaqah*. Allah's Messenger (peace be upon him) said: *"When you smile in your brother's face, or enjoin what is reputable, or forbid what is objectionable, or direct someone who has lost his way, or help a man who has bad eyesight, or remove stones, thorns and bones from the road, or pour water from your bucket into your brother's, it counts to you as Sadaqah."* (Tirmidhi)

To sum up, paying *zakah* and charity purifies a person's wealth. They also purify the heart and soul of the love of material wealth. "Just as ablutions purify the body and *salah* purifies the soul, so *zakah* purifies possessions and makes them pleasing to God" write Sachiko Murata and William C. Chittick while explaining the purification aspect of *zakah* in their book *The Vision of Islam*.[49] Giving charity prolongs a person's life. It causes wealth, reward & blessings to grow manifold. It also saves one from one's own greed and thus makes one more successful. It is a sign of a person's sincerity of faith because wealth is dear to people and something that is loved will not be given up except for something that is more loved. Hence it is called *"sadaqah"*, because in reality it is an indication of the sincerity (sidq) of a person's desire to please Allah. Most importantly, as Prophet Muhammad (peace be upon him) said: *"Sadaqah extinguishes sins as water extinguishes fire."* (Tirmidhi) and in another tradition he said: *"The believer's shade on the Day of Resurrection will be his Sadaqah."* (Tirmidhi)

[49] Murata, Sachiko & Chittick, William C. (1994). *The Vision of Islam*. St. Paul, Minnesota, Paragon House.

CHAPTER FOUR

The Pilgrimage (*Hajj*) – Lessons & Wisdom behind Its Rituals

*H*AJJ LITERALLY MEANS "TO CONTINUOUSLY STRIVE to reach one's goal." In the Islamic teachings, *Hajj* is a form of worship, which involves traveling to the Ka'bah (House of Allah) to carryout certain rituals. It is one of the five pillars of Islam. The other four are a declaration of faith in one God and in Prophet Muhammad (peace be upon him), the five daily prayers, offering regular charity, and fasting the month of Ramadan. *Hajj* or pilgrimage is once-in-a-lifetime obligation for those who have the physical and financial ability to undertake the journey. *Hajj* is a comprehensive form of worship because, on the one hand, it has the qualities of bodily-acts of worship (such as, salah, fasting) and, on the other hand, it carries in it the qualities of the types of worship involving charity (such as zakah (obligatory charity), sadaqah (voluntary charity)). Prophet Muhammad (peace be upon him) said the following words about the virtues of *Hajj*:

> Whosoever performs *Hajj* while having abstained from acts of lewdness, obscenities, and wrangling, shall come home like a newborn (washed clean of sins). (Bukhari & Muslim)

In addition, he said, "*A virtuous Hajj merits no reward other than Paradise*" (Bukhari & Muslim). This chapter is not meant to describe how to perform the *Hajj* rituals based on the Islamic commandments. Instead, the main focus of this chapter is to describe the wisdom under-lying some of the rituals of the *Hajj*.

The main purpose of the *Hajj* is to give direction to a person's life. Prophet Muhammad (peace be upon him) said in a tradition: "*Verily, the real immigrant is the one who immigrates from (leave) sin.*" (Ibn

Habban) From this perspective, the journey for *Hajj* is similar to immigrating to Allah because all the rituals of *Hajj* signify a person's journey from a sinful life to a life of obedience to Allah. And, in fact, our ultimate journey is to Allah as mentioned in the Qur'an: *"and unto Allah is the journeying."* (Surah An-Noor: 42)

WEARING THE *IHRAM*

When the pilgrim puts on the two garments of his *"ihram"*, he cannot help but be reminded of the shroud in which he will be wrapped after he dies. Once he puts on the ihram, his *Hajj* begins and not only is he expected to abstain from sins but also many things which are permissible for him outside the state of ihram become prohibited for him now. This aspect of *Hajj* and its restrictions resemble much like the restrictions in the state of *sawn* (fasting). Putting on the ihram prompts a pilgrim to give up disobedience and misdeeds. Just as he gives up his regular clothing for *Hajj*, likewise he has to give up sins. Just as he has put on two clean, white garments, he has to make his heart clean and pure and abstain from the life of sins and disobedience.

A pilgrim changes his clothes at Miqat. In a way, he experiences death at *Miqat* by putting on the white clothing (*ihram*) and, then, resurrection after which he must continue his journey towards the ground of Arafah, very similar to the gathering of people in Arafah on the day of Judgment. In addition, the pilgrim changes his clothes at *Miqat* to subjugate his ego because, after all, clothes symbolize status and distinction in the society whereas at the time of *Hajj*, people gather in front of Allah free from any social distinction.

TAWAF (CIRCUMAMBULATION) AROUND THE KA'BAH

Tawaf literally means to circumambulate or to revolve around something. In Islamic teachings, *tawaf* refers to walking around the House of Allah (Ka'bah) in a circular pattern. According to the Qur'an, the first house built to worship Allah was the Ka'bah:

"Verily, the first House (of worship) appointed for mankind was that at Bakkah (Makkah), full of blessing, and a guidance for the nations." (Surah Ale-Imran: 96)

When the pilgrims arrive at Makkah, they make the *tawaf* of arrival, which is recommended, not obligatory. After performing the *Tawaf* of arrival, they can make the *Sa'ee* (ritual of running between the mounts of Safa and Marwah) for their *Hajj*. This *Sa'ee* is obligatory and is one of the pillars of *Hajj*, and it can be done either after the *tawaf* of arrival or after the second *tawaf* of *Hajj*.

Performing the *tawaf* is one of the most spiritually uplifting times in the life of a Muslim. It is done seven times in an anti-clockwise manner with the left side of the body facing the Ka'bah. The same anti-clockwise motion can also be observed in nature from the largest scale to the smallest scale. For example, all the planets in our solar system revolve around the sun in an anti-clockwise manner, while electrons also rotate around the nucleus of an atom in the same manner. Similarly, Ka'bah is the center of the Muslim nation. Since Islam is a religion in complete accordance with the human nature, Muslims also circumambulate around the Ka'bah in an anti- clockwise manner. Some Islamic scholars have said that *tawaf* is done in an anti-clockwise manner because in this position the heart (which is towards the left side of the body) is inclining towards the Ka'bah.[50] The human soul, because of its heavenly origins, yearns to meet Allah and so the heart, as the seat of the human soul, inclines towards the Ka'bah symbolising that desire. The Ka'bah also symbolises the Islamic concept of Monotheism. During *tawaf*, Muslims testify that Allah is the centre of existence and He is the focus of our hearts. Commenting on the wisdom behind the *tawaf* of the Ka'bah, Austrian Muslim convert Muhammad Asad (former Leopold Weiss) writes the following in his book Islam at the Crossroads:

---

[50] Mushtaq, Gohar, Ph.D. (2006). *The Intelligent Heart, The Pure Heart: An Insight into the Heart based on Qur'an, Sunnah and Modern Science.* London, Ta-Ha Publishers.

"If we move in a circle around some object we thereby establish that object as the central point of our action. The Ka'bah, towards which every Muslim turns his face in prayer, symbolizes the Oneness of God. The bodily movement of the pilgrims in the *tawaf* symbolizes the activity of human life. Consequently, the *tawaf* implies that not only our devotional thoughts, but also our practical life, our actions and endeavors, must have the idea of God and His Oneness for their center – in accordance with the words of the Holy Qur'an: 'I have not created Jinn and Man but that they should worship Me.' (Surah Dhaariyat: 56)"

It may appear strange for non-Muslims to see the House of Allah as a cube-shaped structure around which people circumambulate. The building of Ka'bah is empty from within to convey a simple message to people about the abstract nature of the concept of Allah in Islam because there is none similar to Him as the Qur'an tells us: *"There is nothing whatever like unto Him"* (Surah Ash-Shoora: 11)

Orientalist Fritz Meier offered an important meditation to his students on the significance of the Ka'bah. He regarded the Ka'bah as "the symbol of antiquity, of a time out of mind" and "a symbol of the pre-existence of God"; and the *kiswa*, the black veil which always shrouds it, is the veil which we must lift it if we are to come to *al-Haqq*, the Real. [51]

When Kazimir Malevich, the Great Russian painter, art theoretician and pioneer of geometric abstract art drew his most famous painting called 'Black Square', he called it the 'absolute symbol of modernity' and the end of all stories. Malevich wrote that when he was painting it, he had felt "a timidity bordering on fear" but when he was about to complete the painting, he experienced a "blissful sensation of being drawn into a desert where nothing is real but feeling, and feeling became the substance of life."[52]

[51] Meier, F. (1955) "The Mystery of the Ka'ba: Symbol and Reality in Islamic Mysticism", in Joseph Campbell (ed.) *The Mysteries: Papers from the Eranos Yearbooks, London*, quoted in: Winter, Tim (2004). "The Chador of God on Earth: the Metaphysics of the Muslim Veil." *New Blackfriars* 85(996): 144-157.

[52] *Quoted in: Winter*, Tim (2004). "The Chador of God on Earth: the Metaphysics of the Muslim Veil." *New Blackfriars* 85(996): 144-157.

British novelist, artist and travel writer, Bruce Chatwin, in his renowned travel-autobiography What am I doing here? offers the following insight about Malevich's painting of the *Black Square*:

"This is not the language of a good Marxist, but of Master Eckhart – or, for that matter, of Mohammad. Malevich's Black Square, his 'absolute symbol of modernity', is the equivalent in painting of the black-draped Ka'bah at Mecca, the shrine in a valley of sterile soil where all men are equal before God." [53]

Islam is a religion for the whole humanity, for the rich and the poor, for everyone. For this reason, the Qur'an begins in the name of God and ends in the name of the people (An-Naas). Similarly, the Ka'bah is called the House of Allah but elsewhere in the Qur'an, it is also called "house of the people" and the "free house" (*al bayt al-ateeq*) as opposed to other houses which have the private ownership. The Ka'bah is the House of God but also the house of people. The Ka'bah represents the freedom of humanity for it is the house free from the sovereignty and ownership of anyone.

Tawaf is performed seven times around the Ka'bah. The figure seven could be symbolic. When we want to measure time, which has no beginning or end, we use the figure seven. There are seven days in a week. The same seven days keep on repeating themselves. The word seven is used as a symbol of perpetuity. If we circumambulate around the Ka'bah seven times, it would be synonymous with the performance of our duty eternally. Dr. Ali Shariati notes in his book *Hajj* that just as there are seven days in a week, going round the Ka'bah seven times represents the eternal struggle which Muslims have to engage in when they are spreading the message of Islam. [54]

In addition to the above-mentioned explanations, there are even deeper wisdoms regarding number seven which have been discovered only recently by the scientists. Modern science has shown that number seven is the most appropriate count for the human brain to remember.

---

[53] Chatwin, Bruce (1990). *What am I doing here?* New York, Penguin.
[54] Shariati, Dr. Ali (1994). *Hajj.* Houston, Free Islamic Literatures, Inc.

Renowned U.S. psychologist from Princeton University George A. Miller published his research findings in the 1956 issue of *The Psychological Review* (vol. 63) under the title "The Magical Number Seven, Plus or Minus Two." One of the things he pointed out in his findings was that the human memory works in such a way that it is easier for the human brain to memorize up to seven chunks of information. In general, it becomes harder for the human brain to remember information chunks beyond seven. Hence, the span of our "immediate memory is "usually somewhere in the neighborhood of seven."[55] For example, it is easier for humans to remember seven types of something. According to Dr. Miller, human nature and intuition might be aware that number seven is most appropriate for it. It could be due to this that we have "the seven wonders of the world, the seven seas, the seven deadly sins, the seven ages of man, the seven levels of hell, the seven notes of the musical scale, and the seven days of the week."[56] Similarly, we have seven colors of the rainbow and seven continents on this earth. Furthermore, Allah created seven heavens as mentioned in the Qur'an: *"Who has created the seven heavens one above another, you can see no fault in the creations of the Most Beneficent. Then look again: 'Can you see any rifts?' "* (Surah Al-Mulk: 3) Since Islam is the religion of human nature, it has chosen number seven in its rituals of *tawaf* and sa'ee in accordance with the nature and limits of the human brain.

LESSONS FROM *SA'EE*

After completing the *tawaf*, a pilgrim is to run between the mounts of Safa and Marwah (it encompasses about ? of a mile), a ritual known as sa'ee. It is obligatory (*wajib*) to begin sa'ee from mount Safa. The Sa'ee is performed seven times between the mounts of Safa and Marwah. By

---

[55] Miller, George A. (1956). "The Magical Number Sever, Plus or Minus Two." *The Psychological Review* 63: 81-97.

[56] Miller, George A. (1956). "The Magical Number Sever, Plus or Minus Two." *The Psychological Review* 63: 81-97.

doing sa'ee seven times, it begins at mount Safa and it ends at mount Marwah (in the case of doing sa'ee six or eight times, it would have ended at the same point it was started from). The ritual of sa'ee is the revivification of the episode of Prophet Abraham (peace be upon him). At Allah's command, he left his wife Hajira and his infant son Ismael in the midst of the desert, close to the mounts of Safa and Marwah. When a pilgrim performs sa'ee, he/she portrays the intensity of a mother's love at Safa and Marwah by running where Hajira had run and by walking with dignity where she had walked in that way. The act of sa'ee not only epitomizes the memory of motherly love but it also symbolizes the unlimited love that the Creator has for His creatures.

The running and walking between the mounts of Safa and Marwah signify the struggle in the human life. Dr. Ali Shariati states in his book *Hajj* that Hajira was merely a slave of Sarah (Abraham's first wife) but she conveyed a great message to all the worldly philosophers, scientists, and great thinkers of the world. Hajira taught them that we must not sit quietly today. Hajira did not sit quietly beside her son. She did not wait "for a miracle to occur or for an invisible hand to bring some fruits from heaven or to flow a river to quench their thirst."[57] She did her part to the best of her abilities in her search for water in the dry mountains of Makkah. Finally, Allah blessed the mother and the son with the miraculous fountain of Zam-zam. Today, the Muslim nation is going through various trials and tribulations but if they follow the example of their great-grand mother Hajira and they struggle to change their condition then Allah will start the fountain of victory for Muslims today just like He started the fountain of Zam-zam for Hajira many centuries ago.

STAYING AT ARAFAT

After performing these rites, the pilgrims proceed to Arafat where they must remain until the sunset of the ninth day. The plain of Arafat is

---

[57] Shariati, Dr. Ali (1994). *Hajj*. Houston, Free Islamic Literatures, Inc.

a vast ground. Making a stay at the plain of Arafat is the major pillar of the *Hajj* so much so that it has been narrated in a Prophetic tradition: "*Hajj* is (staying in) Arafat" (At-Tirmidhi) According to some traditions, the plain of Arafat is the place where Adam and Eve met each other after a long separation which started with their expulsion from Heaven. Allah forgave Adam his trespass. Staying at Arafat reminds the pilgrims to seek forgiveness of Allah just as their great ancestor Prophet Adam did. After all, it has been mentioned in a Prophetic tradition:

> "There is no day in which Allah frees a greater number of His slaves from the Hellfire than the Day of Arafat. Allah comes close to His slaves and boasts about them to the angels, then asks (a rhetorical question): "What do these slaves seek?" (Muslim)

Islamic scholar Abdur Rehman Ibn al-Jawzi (d. 507 H/ 1201 CE) talked about the scene of Arafat in his book *Minhaj ul-Qaasideen*: "The standing of hundreds of thousands of pilgrims in white dress before Allah at the plain of Arafat actually reminds us of the future scene of standing of the whole humanity in front of Allah on the Day of Judgment, a day when everyone will be helpless, hoping for the mercy of Allah."[58]

It was on the occasion of *Hajjatul Wida'a* (The Farewell *Hajj* of Prophet Muhammad peace be upon him) that the following verses of Surah Al-Ma'idah were revealed on the Prophet: *"This day, I have perfected your religion for you, completed My Favor upon you, and have chosen for you Islam as your religion."* (Surah Al-Ma'idah: 3) Just as the day of Arafah is the most important day of *Hajj*, in the same way this verse of Surah Al-Ma'idah is the most important for the Muslim nation until the day of Judgment because, after the revelation of this verse, only Islam is the acceptable religion in the sight of Allah and there is no room for adding any innovation in this religion.

>

---

[58] Ibn al-Jawzee, Imam Abdur Rehman (1992). *Minhajul Qaasideen.* Lahore, Idara Maarif Islami.

CASTING PEBBLES AT SATAN

Ramee refers to the practice in which the pilgrims throw pebbles at three different pillars in Mina during the *Hajj*. It is a *wajib* (obligatory) act in the *Hajj*. According to the Islamic traditions, after seeing the dream on three consecutive days, Prophet Ibrahim (peace be upon him) was taking his son Ismael (peace be upon him) towards Mina for sacrifice to fulfill the commandment of Allah. First, Satan appeared in the guise of a man to waylay Prophet Ibrahim. He tried to cast doubts in Ibrahim's mind by suggesting that Satan might have appeared in the dream he saw. However, Ibrahim, owing to his prophetic vision, immediately recognized Satan and threw some pebbles at him. Satan disappeared immediately but soon reappeared in another form at some distance in front of Hajira, the mother of Ismael. This time he terrified Hajira to prevent her husband from sacrificing their only son. But Hajira also recognized Satan and threw pebbles at him. Then, Satan appeared before the young Ismael and tried to scare him from the pain he would suffer in case of his sacrifice. But Ismael was the member of the same noble family and had the foresight of a prophet. Ismael also threw pebbles at Satan. Today, by emulating the sunnah of the noble family of Prophet Ibrahim (peace be upon him), the pilgrims throw stones at "Satan" at three places. By doing so, the pilgrims are taught the lesson that we must fight back the whispers of Satan we encounter when we carry out the commandments of Allah.

In addition, those three pillars representing the three Satans actually symbolize the three idols or symbols of trinity, which had existed in every age in every religion and which is described in the Qur'an in the form of three historical figures of Pharaoh, Qarun (Korah) and Balam bin Bau'ra. King Pharaoh epitomized political oppression, Qarun represented economic exploitation and Balam personified the hypocrisy of religious scholars. In any oppressive system, the root of evil is always those three Satans, i.e., tyrant rulers, corrupt rich people and evil religious scholars. In the life history of Prophet Muhammad (peace be upon him), those three historical symbols united against Islam were epitomized in the political tyranny of Abu Jahl, in the economic exploitation of Abu Lahb and in the religious hypocrisy of Abdullah Ibn Ubayy. *Hajj* creates awareness in the pilgrims about those three faces of Satan.

LIFE OF PROPHET IBRAHIM – FULL OF TESTS

The pilgrims are commanded to sacrifice animals on the day of Eid al-Adha during the *Hajj*. This act of sacrificing of animals is in fact the ransom for the sacrifice of Ismael as mentioned in the Qur'an: *"And We ransomed him (Ismael) with a great sacrifice (i.e., a ram); And We left for him (a goodly remembrance) among generations (to come) in later times. Salamun (peace) be upon Ibrahim!"* (Surah As-Saffat: 107-109) This is the remembrance of the great incident in which a 100-year old father was asked by Allah to sacrifice his only young son. This can be considered as the landmark incident in history, and, hence, it is referred to as "Sha'airullah" (one of the signs of Allah) in the Qur'an. When the companions asked Prophet Muhammad (peace be upon him): *"O Prophet of Allah! What are these sacrifices of animals at the time of Hajj? Prophet Muhammad replied: "This is the sunnah of your father Ibrahim."* (At-Tirmidhi) Hence, it was Prophet Ibrahim (Abraham) and his son Ismael (peace be upon them) who started the sunnah of sacrifice and it is the followers of Prophet Muhammad (peace be upon him) who will continue it until the Last Day.

If we look at the life of Prophet Ibrahim (peace be upon him), his life was filled with trials and tests from Allah. Prophet Ibrahim passed all of those tests of life with an A+ grade. Finally, Allah made Ibrahim the Imam (leader) of humanity and said about him in the Qur'an:

"And (remember) when the Lord of Ibrahim tried him with certain Commands, which he fulfilled. Allah said to him: "Verily, I am going to make you a leader (Prophet) of humanity." (Surah Al-Baqarah: 124)

The tests and trials in the life of Prophet Ibrahim can be summarized in the following table:

Table: 1

Test & Trials in the Life of Prophet Ibrahim (peace be upon him)

	Description of Test	Type of Test	Result
1	Ibrahim challenged his father and proved that he did not blindly follow the traditions of his forefathers	Test of Love for Traditions of Forefathers	√ Passed
2	Ibrahim challenged the people around him in the society	Test of Love for Friends and Society	√ Passed
3	Ibrahim challenged the king and, as a consequence, he risked his own life. The king threw him in the fire but Allah saved Ibrahim by commanding the fire not to harm Ibrahim.	Test of Love for One's Own Life	√ Passed
4	Ibrahim was commanded by Allah to leave his wife and infant son Ismael in the barren and dry valley of Makkah. It was only after Ibrahim left that Allah blessed the mother and the son with the miraculous fountain of Zam-Zam.	Test of Love for His Wife	√ Passed
5	Ibrahim was commanded by Allah in the dream to sacrifice his only son Ismael	Test of Love for His Children	√ Passed

The last test faced by Prophet Ibrahim was the toughest of all because that was the test of parental love in which a 100-year old father was commanded by Allah to sacrifice his 13-year old son Ismael. The Qur'an testifies to the severity of that test in the following words: *"Verily that indeed was a manifest trial."* (Surah As-Saffat: 106) When Ibrahim had laid down Ismael to give his sacrifice, he heard the voice: *"And We called out to him: "O Abraham! You have fulfilled the dream (vision)!" Verily! Thus do We reward the Muhsinun (good-doers)"* (Surah As-Saffat: 104, 105)

After successfully passing this final test, Prophet Ibrahim reached the stage of Ihsan (highest stage of spirituality) and Allah made him the leader of mankind. There is a great lesson for the believers in the life of Prophet Ibrahim. Every attack of Satan was ineffective against him because Prophet Ibrahim always obeyed Allah and followed the path of righteousness. He never tried to use the rationalizing capabilities of his brain to justify any acts of disobedience to Allah. We must also follow Prophet Ibrahim and must never try to justify a matter that appears appealing to desires of the self (nafs) but it is against the commandments of Allah and His Messenger (peace be upon him).

LIFE OF HAJIRA – A GREAT EXAMPLE FOR MUSLIM WOMEN

The rites and rituals of the *Hajj*, especially sa'ee and ramee and drinking zam-zam water, remind us of Hajira, the wife of Prophet Ibrahim. She decided to stay along with her infant son Ismael in the barren valley of Makkah just for the sake of obeying Allah's command. Allah accepted the sacrificial act of this humble woman and made her the progenitor of a huge nation. Hajira can be regarded as the mother of a great civilization. Hajira was originally from Egypt. Her name means "city" in her mother language. Allah turned Hajira's name into a living reality. Scientists of history and sociology tell us that almost every great civilization originates at a place where there is water. For example, the Indus civilization of the Indian sub-continent, the Egyptian civilization, the Babylonian civilization, etc. had their foundations in the regions having the great rivers of Indus, Nile, and Euphrates, respectively. After all, every living thing originated from water as mentioned in the Qur'an:

> *And We have made from water every living thing. Will they not then believe?"* (Surah Al-Anbiya: 30)

Similarly, the actual beginning of the Arab nation at Makkah happened with the inception of the spring of Zam-zam water, and that happened because of the love of Hajira for her son Ismael and her great tawakkul (trust) in Allah. The first residents of the valley of Makkah were a mother (Hajira) and her son (Ismael). Several years later Prophet Ibrahim came to Makkah to visit his wife and his son. When he reached close to his house in the darkness of the night, he heard his wife reciting Suhuf Ibrahim (The Scriptures of Ibrahim), and she was also teaching those scriptures to her young son Ismael. Upon hearing this, Prophet Ibrahim's heart was filled with joy because his family was so much blessed by Allah.

When the fountain of Zam-zam emanated in the valley of Makkah, the Arab nomad tribe of Jurham reached that location upon seeing the birds flowing above that valley, a sign of the presence of water in that area. They were surprised to find a woman with her infant son, sitting right next to the fountain of Zam-zam. They realized that she must be a blessed woman. They sought Hajira's permission to settle in the valley of Makkah. Later on, when Prophet Ismael grew up, he was married to one of the women from the tribe of Jurham. Hajira lived up to the age of 90. Her blessed presence was a source of inspiration for all in the valley of Makkah. She used to teach and help memorize the Suhuf Ibrahim to the children of Jurham tribe. In addition, she would also teach the children how to write because, according to some narrations, the first person who started writing in Makkah was, in fact, Hajira, the wife of Prophet Ibrahim. [59]

Hence, the center of Arab civilization was Makkah, which was founded by Hajira, and she was the one who taught the art of writing to the Arabs living there. It is through the pen that knowledge is preserved and transferred to succeeding generations. On the level of the human body, modern science tells us that in the womb of the mother, it is the mother's heartbeat which actually jump-starts the heart of the unborn child. Scientist and researcher Paul Pearsall, Ph.D., writes in his book *The Heart's Code* that "the mother's heart energy conveyed in primal sound waves contains the information that is the code that jump-starts our life." [60] Very similarly to this, but on a national level, it was Hajira who

---

[59] Jumuah, Ahmed Khalil (1999). *Wives of the Prophets* (Azwaajul Anbiyaa). Karachi, Darul Isha'at.

[60] Pearsall, Paul Ph.D. (1998). *The Heart's Code*. New York, Broadway Books.

gave a jump-start to the Arabs of Makkah by teaching them how to write, and it was those Arabs who became the Muslim Ummah in later centuries. Hajira is truly regarded as the "Ummul Arab" – the mother of the Arabs, but she was more than a great mother. She was also a great teacher, and from her progeny came the leader of all the prophets – Prophet Muhammad (peace be upon him) – who once said to his companions: "*Verily, I have been sent as a teacher.*" (Ibn Majah)

Indeed, in the life of Hajira, there is a great example for Muslim women. She gave birth and raised a whole civilization, but, in spite of that, her biggest goal in her life was not to search for a career by forsaking the family. Her biggest goal was her role as a mother. Today, the United Nation's social engineering program is attempting, with empty slogans and catchy phrases, to drag Muslim mothers out of their homes so that those mothers do not concentrate on raising Islamic children. The purpose of today's feminist liberation movement is to free women from the "worries" of their homes because feminists know that a mother's love and care for her children raise the best human beings. In fact, it is for this reason that Simone de Beauvoir, the French feminist writer and famous activist in the women's liberation movement, clearly said in a New York Magazine interview (September 1975): "Until the myth of the family, the myth of motherhood and maternal instinct is destroyed, women cannot be liberated."

Today, the success of the Muslim nation lies in following the life example of Hajira, the wife of Prophet Ibrahim. She was one of the greatest women in history. Her only desire in the last part of her life was that when death approaches her, her eyes would be fixed at the Ka'bah, the House of Allah. [61]

PSYCHOLOGICAL IMPACT OF *HAJJ* ON THE PILGRIMS' LIVES

Dr. Malik Badri is a renowned Muslim psychologist from Sudan, who is presently the acting-dean at the International Institute of Islamic Thought and Civilization (ISTAC), Kuala Lumpur, Malaysia. Dr. Badri made various

---

[61] Jumuah, Ahmed Khalil (1999). *Wives of the Prophets (Azwaajul Anbiyaa)*. Karachi, Darul Isha'at.

trips for *Hajj*. In his book *The AIDS Crisis: An Islamic Socio-cultural Perspective*, he sheds light about the effects of *Hajj* on the pilgrims' lives from a psychologist's perspective.[62] Every year, millions of Muslims travel to Makkah to perform the holy rites of the *Hajj*. All the pilgrims visit the holy *Ka'bah* (House of Allah) and carry out specific rituals. They gather in the vast valley of 'Arafah from noon to sunset to engage in prayer, glorifying Almighty Allah and begging His forgiveness. Dr. Badri notes that in spite of all the hardships of travel, overcrowding, and high temperatures, the experiences of *Hajj* and *Umrah* are so moving and spiritually invigorating that most Muslims return to their countries with complete spiritual transformation. Many Muslims make sincere repentance to their sins, never to commit those sins again and pledge to uphold their daily prayers and other religious obligations. The number of Muslims who attend the annual "Islamic convention" of *Hajj* is more than two million. Similarly, the numbers of Muslims who go for *Umrah* and gather to attend the blessed night prayer of the twenty-seventh of Ramadan exceed one million. It is interesting to note that there are no entertainment sessions in these congregations, yet Muslims attend these blessed gatherings after voluntarily paying for their transportation and other travel expenses. In fact, Muslims do not come to these gatherings to amuse themselves. They attend these gatherings with seriousness and humility.

Another interesting fact to bear in mind is that a few decades ago, most Muslims who would go for *Hajj* or *Umrah* were the elderly who desired to carry out these obligations before their death. However, the situation is completely different now. Presently, the major populations of the pilgrims to *Hajj* or the attendants of *Umrah* are young men and women in their thirties, even though youth is a time when people are most vulnerable to worldly temptations. These Muslim men and women attend such Muslim gatherings with elegance and sincerity, and consequently, they reap the fruits of these congregations in the form of new spiritual strength and vigor.

---

[62] Badri, Malik (1997). *The AIDS Crisis: An Islamic Socio-cultural Perspective*. Kuala Lumpur, The International Institute of Islamic Thought and Civilization.

HAJJ EXPERIENCES OF SOME OF THE CONVERTS TO ISLAM

Lastly, *Hajj* experiences of some of the converts to Islam are presented who described what they felt during the mesmerizing *Hajj* journey and its rituals:

(1) Lady Evelyn Zeinab Cobbold

The first British Muslim convert woman who recorded her feelings about her *Hajj* journey was Lady Evelyn Cobbold. She was the daughter of Charles Adolphus Murray (1841-1907), the 7th Earl of Dunmore (Scotland). She embraced Islam on April of 1933. At the age of 66, Lady Cobbold performed the *Hajj*. In 1934, an account of her trip was published entitled Pilgrimage to Mecca (published London, 1934). Lady Cobbold has provided the description of the scene of staying at the plain of Arafat in the following words:

> "It would require a master pen to describe the scene, poignant in its intensity, of that great concourse of humanity of which I was one small unit, completely lost to their surroundings in a fervor of religious enthusiasm. Many of the pilgrims had tears streaming down their cheeks; others raised their faces to the starlit sky that had witnessed this drama so often in the past centuries. The shining eyes, the passionate appeals, the pitiful hands outstretched in prayer moved me in a way that nothing had ever done before, and I felt caught up in a strong wave of spiritual exaltation. I was one with the rest of the pilgrims in a sublime act of complete surrender to the Supreme Will which is Islam.... As I stand beside the granite pillar, I feel I am on Sacred ground. I see with my mind's eye the Prophet delivering that last address, over thirteen hundred years ago, to the weeping multitudes. I visualize the many preachers who have spoken to countless millions who have assembled on the vast plain below; for this is the culminating scene of the Great Pilgrimage."[63]

---

[63] Nawwab, Ni'mah Isma'il (July-August 1992) *ARAMCO World* (Dhahran, Saudi Arabia).

(2) Mohammad Asad (Leopold Weiss)

Mohammad Asad was an Austrian Jew, who accepted Islam in the year 1926. Between 1927 and 1932, he performed *Hajj* five times. He writes the memoirs of the enthralling experience of *Hajj* in his book *The Road to Mecca:*

"And as I stand on the hillcrest and gaze down toward the invisible Plain of 'Arafat, the moonlit blueness of the landscape before me, so dead a moment ago, suddenly comes to life with the currents of all the human lives that have passed through it and is filled with the eerie voices of the millions of men and women who have walked or ridden between Mecca and 'Arafat in over thirteen hundred pilgrimages for over thirteen hundred years. Their voices and their steps and the voices and the steps of their animals reawaken and resound anew; I see them walking and riding and assembling—all those myriads of white-garbed pilgrims of thirteen hundred years; I hear the sounds of their passed-away days; the wings of the faith which has drawn them together to this land of rocks and sand and seeming deadness beat again with the warmth of life over the arc of centuries, and the mighty wing beat draws me into its orbit and draws my own passed-away days into the present, and once again I am riding over the plain—riding in a thundering gallop over the plain, amidst thousands, and thousands of Ihram-clad Bedouins, returning form 'Arafat to Mecca.... and the wind shouts a wild paean [song or hymn] of joy into my ears: 'Never again, never again, never again will you be a stranger!'" [64]

After completing the *Hajj* at Makkah, pilgrims also try to seize the opportunity provided by the *Hajj* to visit the Prophet's Mosque in Madinah, where the Prophet (peace be upon him) lies buried in a simple grave under the green dome of the mosque. Although the visit to Madinah is not part of the *Hajj*, but the city - which welcomed Prophet

---

[64] Asad, Muhammad (2002). *The Road to Mecca*. Malaysia, Islamic Book Trust.

Muhammad (peace be upon him) when he migrated there from Makkah
- is rich in providing us with the memories of our Holy Prophet.
Muhammad Asad while unfolding his *Hajj* journey describes his feelings
in Madinah:

> "Even after thirteen centuries [the Prophet's] spiritual presence is
> almost as alive here as it was then. It was only because of him that
> the scattered group of villages once called Yathrib became a city
> and has been loved by all Muslims down to this day as no city
> anywhere else in the world has ever been loved. It has not even a
> name of its own: for more than thirteen hundred years it has been
> called Madinat an-Nabi, 'the City of the Prophet.' For more than
> thirteen hundred years, so much love has converged here that all
> shapes and movements have acquired a kind of family resem-
> blance, and all differences of appearance find a tonal transition
> into a common harmony." [65]

(3) Malcolm X (El-Hajj Malik El-Shabbaz)

One of the most celebrated Western pilgrims is the African-American
civil rights leader El-Hajj Malik El-Shabbaz, more commonly known as
Malcolm X. He was the man who was well-known for his preaching that
whites were "devils." However, Malcolm X seriously reassessed his racist
views during his pilgrimage to Makkah in 1964. He embraced Islam at
the hands of King Faisal of Saudi Arabia. As a result of this spiritual transformation after the *Hajj*, he bid farewell to the Black nationalist movement of the Nation of Islam. After the *Hajj* while he was still in Makkah,
Malcolm X wrote a letter to his students, which was later published in his
book *The Autobiography of Malcolm X*. In this letter, Malcolm writes:

> "There were tens of thousands of pilgrims, from all over the
> world. They were of all colors, from blue-eyed blondes to black-
> skinned Africans. But we were all participating in the same ritu-
> al, displaying a spirit of unity and brotherhood that my experi-

---

[65] Ibid

ences in America had led me to believe never could exist between the white and non-white."

"America needs to understand Islam, because this is the one religion that erases from its society the race problem. Throughout my travels in the Muslim world, I have met, talked to, and even eaten with people who in America would have been considered white - but the white attitude was removed from their minds by the religion of Islam. I have never before seen sincere and true brotherhood practiced by all colors together, irrespective of their color."

"You may be shocked by these words coming from me. But on this pilgrimage, what I have seen, and experienced, has forced me to rearrange much of my thought-patterns previously held, and to toss aside some of my previous conclusions."

"During the past eleven days here in the Muslim world, I have eaten from the same plate, drank from the same glass, and slept on the same rug - while praying to the same God - with fellow Muslims, whose eyes were the bluest of blue, whose hair was the blondest of blond, and whose skin was the whitest of white. And in the words and in the deeds of the white Muslims, I felt the same sincerity that I felt among the black African Muslims of Nigeria, Sudan and Ghana."[66]

Upon returning to America, Malcolm X embarked on a mission to enlighten both blacks and whites with his new views. Malcolm X recognized that in order to truly learn from the *Hajj*, its inherent spiritual lessons must be extended not only to Muslims but also to people of every faith.

(4) Hamza Yusuf Hanson

Sheikh Hamza Yusuf Hanson was born in Washington State and raised in Northern California. In 1977, he accepted Islam and then traveled to the Muslim world and studied for ten years in the United Arab Emirates, Saudi Arabia, as well as North and West Africa. After ten years

---

[66] X, Malcolm (1992). *The Autobiography of Malcolm X.* New York, Ballantine Books.

of studies abroad, he returned to the USA and took degrees in Religious Studies and Health Care. He is the founder of Zaytuna Institute (California) which is dedicated to the revival of traditional study methods and the sciences of Islam. He explained his *Hajj* experience as described in Steven Barboza's book *American Jihad: Islam After Malcolm X*:

> The first time I made *Hajj* was overwhelming. I saw it ultimately as an intimate experience with the human race, because all of a sudden you see the commonality of mankind....
>
> The Prophet said that this world is a prison for the believer, and it's the paradise of the one who rejects the truth. So for the Muslims – that's his despair. He's is chained in this body and this ego, this self that is constantly calling him to the lowest aspects of himself. And the nafs – I love that term. The nafs, the lower self, is taking us down and the spirit is journeying to break free of that bondage of the nafs. And so *Hajj* is kind of the ultimate manifestation of that intense desire to free oneself of this world and enter a state of purity.
>
> The *Hajj* strips away all that cultural garb. Everybody's dressed the same. You strip away that cultural garb, jettison all that baggage, and there you are with two sheets of cloth, unsewn, the women dressed in white, before God, and you see the man next to you is no different from you, no matter what his color." [67]

(5) Michael Wolfe

Michael Wolfe is an American poet, author, and the President and Executive Producer of Unity Productions Foundation (Educational Media Foundation). Born of a Christian mother and a Jewish father, Michael Wolfe eventually accepted Islam. Wolfe is famous for hosting the award-winning televised account of the *Hajj* from Mecca on ABC's

---

[67] Barboza, Steven (1993). *American Jihad: Islam After Malcolm X*. New York, Doubleday Dell Publishing Group.

"Nightline" as well as *Hajj* documentary for CNN international. He describes his *Hajj* experience, during his pilgrimage to Makkah in 1990, in one of his articles in the following words:

> "The walk around the Ka'ba—the black stone block in the great mosque—is an expression of our desire to put God at the center of our lives…. On the plain of Arafat, we perform the central obligation of the pilgrimage, to be here together from noon until sunset. There is no ceremony. We stroll, we pray, we meditate. The *Hajj* goes on inside the hearts and thoughts of each of us. This is a rehearsal for that Day of Judgment. How will we account for our acts? Have I injured anyone? Have I been grateful enough for the simple gifts of life, water, food, friends, family and the air I breathe? Before leaving Mecca, we visit the Ka'ba one last time. For most of us, this will be our last glimpse of the shrine. There is an old proverb—before you visit Mecca, it beckons you. When you leave it behind, it calls you forever."[68]

---

[68] Wolfe, Michael. *An American in Makkah: The Hajj experience of convert Michael Wolfe.* www.islamfortoday.com/wolfe4.htm.

CHAPTER FIVE

The Linguistic and Historical Miracles of the Qur'an

"All the prophets were gicen such miracles which inspired people to believe. And the miracle that I have been given is the Qur'an." (Sahih Bukahri)

THESE ARE THE WORDS OF PROPHET Muhammad (peace be upon him), which were recorded more than fourteen centuries ago. What are those elements of the Qur'an that make it a living miracle and the word of God? The purpose of this chapter is to highlight some of the miraculous aspects of the Qur'an, which in turn may provide an impetus to non-Muslim readers to study the Qur'an themselves. This is the Book about which Prophet Muhammad (peace be upon him) said in another tradition:

"Repetition does not wear it out, and its wonders do not end. It is the Truth. It is not a jest." (At-Tirmidhi)

CHALLENGE TO MAKE ONE CHAPTER LIKE THE QUR'AN

When the Qur'an was revealed to Prophet Muhammad (peace be upon him) fourteen centuries ago, it gave a challenge to all human beings to produce a book, or even a chapter, that is comparable to the Qur'an:

"And if you are in doubt concerning that which We have sent down (i.e., the Qur'an) to Our servant (Muhammad, peace be upon him), then produce one chapter comparable to it and call your witnesses or helpers (if there are any) besides Allah, if what you say be true." (Surah Al-Baqarah: 23)

It is important to note that this challenge has not been met till this day. No human author can propound such a claim because he/she will know that sooner or later some other author will produce a piece of writing better than the author who made such a claim. The fact that this challenge was given by the Qur'an and no one has been able to meet this challenge is sufficient proof of the Divine origin of the Qur'an.

History tells us that the unmatched literary style of the Qur'an had mesmerizing influence not only on the common people but also the most eloquent poets and orators during the time of Prophet Muhammad (peace be upon him). For example, 'Umar bin al-Khattab was one of the few most educated Makkan Arabs who also knew how to write. When he heard the verses of Surah Ta-Ha recited to him from the Qur'an while he was in his sister's home, he could not resist the irresistible charm of the Qur'an and immediately embraced Islam. Walid ibn al-Mughirah, another leader in Makkah, who personified the eloquence of the literary pride of his period, expressed his opinion concerning the "literary miracle of the Qur'an." When Abu Jahl asked him about his opinion of the Qur'an, Walid replied: "What do I think of it? By God, I think there is nothing of its like... it is too majestic to be matched!" (*Al-Itteqan fi Ulum al-Qur'an* by Sayyuti)[69]

Jubayr ibn Mut'im, a polytheist from Makkah who had not embraced Islam yet, came to visit Medina and he said, "I heard the Prophet (peace be upon him) reciting Surah at-Tur (a chapter in the Qur'an) in the Maghrib (evening) prayer. When he reached the verse of the Qur'an, 'Or were they created out of nothing, or are they the creators? Or did they create the heavens and the earth? No, in truth they have no certainty. Or do they possess the treasuries of your Lord or do they have control of them?' (Surah At-Tur: 35-37), upon hearing those verses, my heart practically flew to Islam." (Bukhari - Kitaab at-Tafseer)

Labid ibn Rabiyah was one of the seven most famous poets of the time and a contemporary of Prophet Muhammad (peace be upon him).

---

[69] Sayyuti, Imam Jalaluddin (1982). *Al-Itteqan fi Ulum al-Qur'an*. Lahore, Idara Islaamiyat.

He was so eloquent that once, when he recited one of his poems at the famous annual gathering of Ukaaz, the other poets fell in prostration before him because they were so much spellbound by the literary eloquence of his verses. Once he wrote a poem in reply to the challenge of the Qur'an that was displayed in public. After a few days, one Muslim brought a Surah from the Qur'an and hung it besides Labid's poem. The next day when Labid, who had not yet embraced Islam, came to that place and read those verses of the Qur'an, he was deeply impressed by the literary excellence of the Qur'an and declared that it must be the work of someone superior to human beings. Not only did Labid immediately accepted Islam, but he was so much overwhelmed by the majesty of the Qur'an that he decided to give up writing poetry altogether. Once he was asked by Umar bin Khattab, the second caliph of Muslims, to recite a poem. Labid replied: "When God has given me such compositions as Surah Al-Baqarah and Surah Ale-Imran (Chapters 2 & 3 - Qur'an), it does not befit me to recite poems." (*Al-Istee'ab* by Ibn Abdul Barr)

HISTORICAL AUTHENTICITY OF THE QUR'AN

In the Qur'an, Allah says:

"We have, without doubt, sent down the Message (i.e., the Qur'an) and surely, We will guard it (from corruption)" (Surah Al-Hijr: 9)

Among all the religious scriptures throughout history, only the Qur'an has the unique characteristic that it has been transferred from generations to generations in the oral as well as written form, from cover to cover, without the slightest change. Committing the Qur'an to memory and writing it down started right from the time when the Qur'an's revelation began on Prophet Muhammad (peace be upon him). Muslim historians note that whenever a revelation was received, the Prophet (peace be upon him) would dictate the text to one of his literate companions. Immediately after dictation, he would ask the scribe to read out what he had written down to ensure accuracy. After dictating, the Prophet (peace be upon him) would ask his companions to memorize the text of the revealed part of the Qur'an and repeat it in the daily prayers. In this way, after the five prayers were ordained, it became easy for the Companions to preserve the verses in their memory when they would recite them five times a day. When Prophet Muhammad (peace be upon him) delivered his farewell sermon on the occasion of Hujjatul Widaa (The Last Pilgrimage), about two and half months before his death, there were one-hundred forty thousand pilgrims present on the plain of Arafat. All those Companions contributed in the historical preservation of the Qur'an. No other prophet before Prophet Muhammad (peace be upon him) had such a large population of their companions in their respective life times to preserve the Divine message of their time. A few years after the death of the Prophet, Uthman bin Affan, the third righteous-guided caliph, unified Muslims on a single dialect of the Qur'an so that the dialectical diversity should not become a cause of disharmony in the Muslim community. Since that time until today, after the passage of more than 1400 years, the Qur'an has been transmitted from generation to generation in a single and unique form from the borders of Morocco to the frontiers of Manchuria.

Among the religious scriptures, the Bible is considered the second most authentic book after the Qur'an. And yet we see that religious historians such as French researcher Professor Eduoard Monet analyzed and questioned the historical authenticity of the Bible. In his book *Histoire de La Bible* (published Paris, 1924 CE), Professor Monet questioned the authenticity of the whole Bible with the exception of 'The Book of Jeremiah'. We as Muslims do not believe in such a harsh criticism on any religious scripture but the historical authenticity of the Bible has been questioned by several other Christian history scholars and philosophers. On the other hand, Qur'an has been preserved not only in writing but also as an oral book. Around the world it is not uncommon to see Muslim children as young as 9 years and sometimes even 7 years old who are 'Haafiz' of the Qur'an – who have memorized the whole Qur'an verbatim from cover to cover. In the words of a French Orientalist, the memorization of the Qur'an from cover to cover provided a unique way of "double checking" the authenticity of the Qur'an when it is transferred from generation to generation.

Dr. Mohammad Hamidullah, an Islamic researcher and a well-known figure in the circles of Orientalists, has mentioned an important research conducted at the Munich University of Germany in an Institute of Quranic Research established there in the early 1900's. According to Dr. Hamidullah, the goal of that Institute was to collect all the oldest available copies of the Holy Qur'an, whether they are in original or as photocopies. This process of collection lasted for three generations. While Dr. Hamidullah was at the University of Paris in 1933, the third Director of the Institute, Mr. Pretzl, came to Paris to get photocopies of all the ancient manuscripts of the Holy Qur'an available in the Public Library of Paris. Professor Pretzl personally told him that at the time (in the year 1933) the institute had 43,000 photocopies of the Holy Qur'an and that their research was still proceeding. Although the institute, its library and staff were all destroyed by a bomb during the Second World War, an interim report was published shortly before the beginning of the Second World War and it stated that the work of collation of the Quranic manuscripts had not yet been completed. But the result of the examination conducted until then stated that in the thousands of manuscripts of the Qur'an, "not a single discrepancy in the text had been discovered." [70]

All this bear testimony to the Divine claim in the Qur'an: "Verily, it is We (Allah) Who revealed the Remembrance (Qur'an) and verily We will guard it (from corruption)." (Surah Al-Hijr: 9)

QUR'AN – NOT A BOOK WRITTEN BY PROPHET MUHAMMAD (PEACE BE UPON HIM)

People who do not believe in the Qur'an as a Divine Book tend to think that the Qur'an was authored by Prophet Muhammad (peace be upon him). However, it is the miracle of the Qur'an that in it lie all the answers to the objections of the people who do not believe in the Qur'an.

---

[70] Hamidullah, Dr. Mohammad (1995). *The Emergence of Islam*. Delhi, Adam Publishers.

Any non-Muslim who opens up the Qur'an and reads it with an objective mind will surely notice that the Qur'an talks very little about the personality of Prophet Muhammad (peace be upon him) himself. Similarly, if we look at the biography of Prophet Muhammad (peace be upon him), we read that the death of his beloved wife, Khadija, and his uncle, Abu Talib, were heart-breaking incidents in the life of Prophet Muhammad (peace be upon him) so much so that the Prophet did not forget his late wife Khadija until he breathed his last. However, we do not see the slightest mention of those two incidents or even the names of those two personalities in the Qur'an. Human moods and emotions – love and hate, friendship and enmity all have their influence upon the human thought. It is not uncommon for such feelings to creep into the writings of the most objective writer. The only one who is free of all such caprice and all such limitations is the Almighty God. For this reason, any unprejudiced reader of the Qur'an will notice in the Qur'an complete absence of any influence of the personal life or emotions of Prophet Muhammad (peace be upon him).

There are verses in the Qur'an addressing the Prophet, which clearly indicate that this Qur'an was revealed by a higher authority on the Prophet. For example, at the onset of Surah Yusuf (Chapter 12) in the Qur'an, Allah addresses Prophet Muhammad (peace be upon him) as follows: *"We relate unto you (Muhammad) the best of stories through Our Revelations unto you, of this Qur'an. And before this (i.e., before the coming of Divine Inspiration to you), you were among those who knew nothing about it (the Qur'an)."* (Surah Yusuf: 3)

Historically, the Qur'an was revealed quite a few times against the personal inclinations of Prophet Muhammad (peace be upon him). For example, six or more times the Prophet's companion Umar bin Khattab disagreed with Prophet Muhammad (peace be upon him) and, later, the Quranic verses were revealed supporting Umar's position. In fact, the very experience of the revelation on Prophet Muhammad (peace be upon him) was no less than a huge burden on him – something about which the Qur'an itself alludes to:

"Verily, We shall send down to you a weighty Word." (Surah Al-Muzzammil: 5)

What is this weighty Word? It is that of the whole Qur'an, as it was to be completed over a period of 23 years of the prophethood of Prophet Muhammad (peace be upon him), as it was revealed on him from Allah by the Angel Gabriel. In one prophetic tradition, one of the companions described: "The revelation came to him in the coldest day, and when it ceased, the front of the Prophet perspired with (sweat falling as) pearls." (Bukhari) Another series of reports say that he then felt the weight of a great load, and said, "I saw the Prophet while he was on his camel when a revelation came to him. The camel began to foam with rage and twist its legs to the point that I feared that they would break with a crack. In fact sometimes the camel sat down, but sometimes it would obstinately try to stand, with legs planted like pegs all through the time of revelation, and this lasted until the state (of revelation) vanished, and sweat would fall from him like pearls." (Ibn Sa'd)[71] Hence, it is clear that the revelation was an awe-inspiring experience for the Prophet. He felt physically crushed by it and was emotionally overpowered by the weight and majesty of the message.

Certain chapters of the Qur'an begin with certain abbreviated letters (huroof Muqatti'at), also known as 'the Imponderables'. If we search all the books containing the ahadeeth or the traditions uttered by Prophet Muhammad (peace be upon him), we will not find a single Prophetic tradition containing such abbreviated letters as they appear in the Qur'an. Moreover, if we just compare the Quranic Arabic language with the Arabic language found in the traditions of Prophet Muhammad (peace be upon him), we can easily notice that the language of the Qur'an is far more eloquent than any human speech. Indeed, the revelation of the Qur'an in Arabic language itself is no less than a miracle as the Qur'an declares:

---

[71] Ibn Sa'd, Abu Abdullah Muhammad (n.d.). *Kitab Al-Tabaqat Al-Kabir.* New Delhi, Kitab Bhavan.

"Surely, We have sent it down as an Arabic Qur'an, in order that you may learn wisdom." (Surah Yusuf: 2)

Before the revelation of the Qur'an, there was no book in the Arabic language. Arabs were oral people with brilliant memories. The first book in the Arabic language was the Qur'an - "Al-Kitaab" (the Book) as it is rightly said in the Qur'an itself: *"This is the Book; in it is guidance sure, without doubt."* (Surah Al-Baqarah: 2)

Before Islam, the Arabs were a nation of *Ummiyeen* (illiterate people) and yet this Book laid the foundations of the most literary civilization the world had ever seen. Qur'an turned the Arabic language into an international language and Islamic civilization into a universal civilization. According to the classification of the United Nations, there are 3,000 languages in this world today. Out of these, only 78 are in written form. Out of these, only 8 are universally used. They have their literature universally read and the Arabic language is one of those 8 universal languages. Qur'an took a nation of illiterates and made them one of the most literate nations of the world. This was the strength of the Quranic Arabic. Titus Burckhardt, a German-Swiss philosopher, writes in his book *Art of Islam: Language and Meaning* about the Quranic Arabic and its impact on Arab civilization:

> *"In Arabic, the 'tree' of verbal forms, of derivatizations from certain roots, is quite inexhaustible; it can always bring forth new leaves, new expressions to represent hitherto dormant variations of the basic idea – or action. This explains why this Bedouin tongue was able to become the linguistic vehicle of an entire civilization very rich and differentiated."*[72]

CONCLUDING REMARKS

Anyone who is objectively studying the Qur'an will discover that even if we put aside myriads of scientific miracles mentioned in the Qur'an, its

---

[72] Burckhardt, Titus (1976). *Art of Islam: Language and Meaning.* London, Islamic Festival Trust Ltd.

linguistic and historical miracles are enough to convince any unprejudiced reader of the Divine origin of the Qur'an. Centuries have passed and the challenges of the Qur'an have yet to be answered. No one has found any discrepancy in it. In fact, the Qur'an provides man with a chance to verify its authenticity and "prove it wrong" in the followings majestic words:

> *"Do they not consider the Qur'an? Had it been from any other than Allah, they would surely have found therein much discrepancy."* (Surah An-Nisa, 4:82)

CHAPTER SIX

Early-Hour Prayers (*Tahajjud*): A Religious-Scientific Perspective

THE WORD "*TAHAJJUD*" IS DERIVED FROM "*Hujud*", meaning to get up from sleep. In Islamic teachings, *tahajjud* prayers mean giving up sleep for offering the optional late-night (pre-dawn) prayers. *Tahajjud* prayers were observed by the Holy Prophet (peace be upon him) from midnight up to the appearance of the early dawn. This prayer was specially ordained for the Holy Prophet (peace be upon him) by the following verses:

"And during a part of the night, pray Tahajjud beyond what is incumbent on you; maybe your Lord will raise you to a position of great glory." (Surah Al-Isra': 79)

Hence, the Prophet was asked to stand up in prayer at night and seek nearness to Allah. This prayer comprises of a minimum of two *rak'ahs* (units). (*Ibn Habban; Targheeb wa tarheeb*) On average, it has four rak'ahs and maximum it has eight *rak'ahs*. Allah has promised great rewards and merits for those who pray *tahajjud*. Among the voluntary prayers (*nawaafil*), this has the most reward. (Muslim; Tirmidhi; Abu Dawud) In the Qur'an, it has been said about this prayer:

"As to the Righteous, they will be in the midst of Gardens and Springs, taking joy in the things which their Lord gives them, because, before then, they lived a good life. They were in the habit of sleeping but little by night, And in the hours of early dawn, they (were found) praying for Forgiveness." (Surah Az-Zaariyat: 15-18)

Similarly, in Surah Al-Furqan, Allah describes those praying *tahajjud* as follows:

"And the servants of (Allah) Most Gracious are those who walk on the earth in humility, and when the ignorant address them, they say, "Peace!" And who spend the night before their Lord, prostrate and standing." (Surah Al-Furqan: 63, 64

Abdullah ibn Salaam reported:

"When the Prophet (peace and blessings be upon him) came to Madinah, the people gathered around him and I was one of them. I looked at his face and understood that it was not the face of a liar. The first words I heard him say were: 'O people, spread the salutations, feed the people, keep the ties of kinship, and pray during the night while the others sleep, and you will enter Paradise in peace.'" (At-Tirmidhi)

One should begin *tahajjud* prayers with two quick rak`ahs and one may pray whatever one wishes after that. Ayesha, the wife of the Prophet (peace be upon him), said:

"When the Prophet prayed during the late-night, he would begin his Prayers with two quick rak`ahs." (Muslim)

It is recommended that one wake up one's family, for Abu Hurairah quoted the Prophet (peace be upon him) as saying:

"May Allah bless the man who gets up during the night to pray and wakes up his wife and who, if she refuses to get up, sprinkles water on her face. And may Allah bless the woman who gets up during the night to pray and wakes up her husband and who, if he refuses, sprinkles water on his face."(Ahmad)

The immense reward for *tahajjud* prayers can be judged from a Prophetic tradition:

"In the Paradise there are rooms the outside of which can be seen from within and the inside from without which Allah has prepared for those who speak gently, provide food, observe frequent fast, and pray during the night when people are asleep." (Bayhaqi in Shu'ab al-Imaan; Tirmidhi)

HOURS OF EARLY DAWN – BEST TIME FOR REPENTANCE

The hours of early dawn are the best time for a person to seek Allah's forgiveness. It is for this reason that it is best to delay this Prayer to the last third portion of the night. Abu Hurairah quoted the Messenger of Allah (peace be upon him) as saying:

> *"Our Lord descends to the lowest heaven during the last third of the night, inquiring: 'Who will call on Me so that I may respond to him? Who is asking something of Me so I may give it to him? Who is asking for My forgiveness so I may forgive him?'"* (Sahih Bukhari)

Similarly, Amr ibn Absah reported that he heard the Prophet (peace be upon him) saying:

> *"The closest that a slave comes to his Lord is during the latter portion of the night. If you can be among those who remember Allah the Exalted One at that time, then do so."* (At-Tirmidhi)

Salman Al-Farsi quoted the Prophet (peace be upon him) as saying:

> *"Observe the night Prayer; it was the practice of the righteous before you and it brings you closer to your Lord and it is penance for evil deeds and erases the sins and repels disease from the body."* (At-Tabarani)

The time of early dawn prayers is the time of self-reckoning. It is the best time for a person to feel remorse for his/her past sinful life. All human beings commit sins and the best of them are the ones who repent. Allah tells us in the Qur'an:

> *"O you who believe! Turn to Allah with sincere repentance! It may be that your Lord will remit from you your sins, and admit you into Gardens under which rivers flow (Paradise)."* (Surah At-Tahrim: 8)

Our ability to mentally recall our past life and deeds is at its climax in the hours of early dawn as it has been shown by modern scientific research. Various scientific experiments conducted both on humans and animals have demonstrated that consolidation of memory occurs during sleep. In a study published in the November 2003 issue of the *European Journal of Neuroscience* (Vol. 18) at the Leibniz Institute for Neurobiology, Brenneckestr (Germany), it was shown that sleep improved memory retention in rats.[73] Deep sleep caused enhancement of memory process in the brain. Similarly, another study conducted by the researchers from the Massachusetts Institute of Technology and recently published in the December 18th issue of *Nature Neuroscience* has shown that the hippocampus, which initially records information while awake, rewinds and replays its stored data at night and passes it along to the neocortex of our brain while we are sleeping.[74] The neocortex is thought to be the long-term home of memories, and is also the place where higher order thinking takes place. Hence, slumber increases the concentrating ability of the memory components of the brain and helps us to recall and review our previous life in order to change for the better. Therefore, when a person gets up from his sleep in the tranquil and dark hours of early dawn, performs *Tahajjud* prayers, and raises his hands in supplication to seek Allah's forgiveness, it is easier for the person to recall his past sins and repent to Allah for his previous shortcomings and transgressions. He/she sheds tears of remorse in front of Allah for his/her previous wrongdoings, sincerely repents and seeks Allah's mercy and forgiveness. The Qur'an describes such people as follows:

> *"Those who show patience, Firmness and self-control; who are true (in word and deed); who worship devoutly; who spend (in the way of Allah); and who pray for forgiveness in the early hours of the morning."* (Surah Ale-Imran: 17)

---

[72] Wetzel, W., Wagner, T. & Balschun, D. (2003). " REM sleep enhancement induced by different procedures improves memory retention in rats." *European Journal of Neuroscience* 18(9): 2611-2617.

[73] Ji, Daoyun & Wilson, Matthew A. (2007) "Coordinated memory replay in the visual cortex and hippocampus during sleep" *Nature Neuroscience* 10, 100 - 107

The timing of *tahajjud* prayers is filled with an atmosphere of spirituality and purity of thought, which gives a spiritual boost to a person for the rest of the day. That is the best time for framing and formulating the wordings of prayer. The person experiences a feeling of being special while he/she is in communion with the Creator of this Universe. This instills a sense of God-consciousness in the person, which is the whole idea of Islamic worship. Love for Allah grows with time, being a slow process and worshipping in the early hours of dawn strengthens this bond between a human being and his Lord. However, one must abstain from unlawful (haram) means or source of earnings in order to benefit from any form of Islamic worship. Unlawful means of earnings very quickly destroy our *Imaan* (faith). *Tahajjud* prayers and shedding tears of repentance at that time are only beneficial if a person uses lawful means to earn his livelihood for his family and to fulfill the financial responsibility of others. Prophet Muhammad (peace be upon him) said in a tradition:

"The man with an unkempt hair and is dust-covered who is on a long journey. He raised up his hands to the heaven (in supplication) saying: 'O my Lord! O my Lord!' While sources of his food, drink and cloth are haram and he is nourished by haram. How then could his supplication be accepted?" (Sahih Muslim)

MEDICAL BENEFITS OF WAKING UP FOR *TAHAJJUD* PRAYERS

There is no doubt that a person saying *tahajjud* prayers gets all the medical benefits which are gained while saying the rest of the obligatory prayers. For example, exercise of the muscles and joints of the body during standing and bowing down, flowing of extra blood supply to the facial muscles and the brain during prostration, drainage of sinuses and, hence, fewer chances of a person getting sinusitis (inflammation of the sinuses). During the night's sleep, the breathing process is slow due to which only two thirds of the capacity of the lung is exhaled out, the remaining one third remains in the lungs as residual air. During prostration, the muscles beneath the lungs are pressed and as a consequence, the remaining one-third residual air has the chance to be expelled out, which is important for healthy lungs. There are less chances of having diseases of the lungs.[75]

However, there are certain other benefits, which are specific to getting up in the hours of the early dawn for *Tahajjud* prayers. Prophet Muhammad (peace be upon him) accentuated the importance of early rising in one *hadeeth* when he said: *"The early morning has been blessed for my Ummah (nation)."* (Sahih al-Jaami, 2841) Similarly, in another tradition, Salman Al-Farsi quoted the Prophet (peace be upon him) as saying:

"Observe the night Prayer; it was the practice of the righteous before you and it brings you closer to your Lord and it is penance for evil deeds and erases the sins and repels disease from the body." (At-Tabarani)

The companion of the Prophet (peace be upon him) who narrated this tradition was Salman Al-Farsi. He himself strictly acted upon this Prophetic commandment of performing the *Tahajjud* prayers regularly so much so that he lived a very long and healthy life. According to certain narrations, Salman Al-Farsi lived for about 150 years and according to some other narrations 250 years. Ibn Hajar al-Asqalani noted in his book *Al-asabah fi tamiz as-Sahaabah* that Salman Al-Farsi died at the age of 250. Even if we accept the narration stating that Salman Al-Farsi lived for about 150 years, this shows that a very healthy life contributed towards Salman Al-Farsi's longevity.

There is no doubt that getting up for the *Tahajjud* prayers repels diseases from our body. When a person wakes up early in the morning, the accumulated body fluids in the form of urine and stools have the opportunity to be excreted out of the body earlier as compared to a person who wakes up late. If urine stays in the body for long period of

---

[75] Discover Islam TV Series "The Daily Prayer (Medical Benefit of Prayer)" Dr. Zakir Naik interviewed by Dr. Linda Thayer

time, it puts unnecessary pressure on the kidneys to do more work. In addition, breathing in the clean and fresh morning air is beneficial for the lungs and brain. It is for this reason that famous American thinker, politician and scientist, Benjamin Franklin wrote the following wise words in his book *Poor Richard's Almanac*:

"Early to bed and early to rise makes a man healthy, wealthy and wise."

It is true that sleep is important for proper functioning of our body. Qur'an tells us: *"And (Allah) made your sleep for rest."* (Surah An-Naba: 9) Sleep provides strength to our body and mind. Complete lack of sleep results in loss of attentiveness, fatigue and illness. However, Islam teaches us to exercise moderation in sleep. Islam teaches us to sleep in the early part of the night and get up on the last part of the night. Our Holy Prophet (peace be upon him) used to sleep for a part of the night and in the hours of the early dawn, he would get up and perform ablution and stood up for the *tahajjud* prayer (Sahih al-Bukhari). Recent scientific research is testifying that the practice of Prophet Muhammad (peace be upon him) is the best routine for many people to follow.

It has been demonstrated by some scientists that sleeping less than 8 hours a day is perfectly healthy for the human body. In the Feb. 14, 2002 issue of WebMD Medical News, Daniel J. DeNoon reported a six-year study conducted on more than a million Americans which demonstrated that a good night's sleep lasts seven hours. It was also shown in the study that people who sleep for eight hours or more tend to die a bit sooner.

The investigating head scientist Daniel F. Kripke, MD, a professor of psychiatry at the University of California, San Diego and his fellow scientists evaluated data from an American Cancer Society study conducted between the years 1982 and 1988. The study collected information on people's sleep habits and health, and then followed them for six years. The ages of study participants ranged from 30 to 102 years, with an average starting age of 57 years for women and 58 years for men. In the study, the risk of death over six years went up 12% for people who slept eight hours, 17% for those who slept nine hours, and 34% for those who slept 10 hours a night. On the other hand, for people who went with too little sleep, the risk of death went up only by 8% for those who slept six hours and only by 11% for those who slept five hours a night. Too much sleep could in fact be harmful for our health. Dr. Kripke noted: "For 10-hour sleepers, the increased risk of death was about the same as that for moderate obesity." The study's main finding, in the words of Dr. Kripke, is as follows: "You really don't have to sleep for eight hours and you don't have to worry about it. It is evidently very safe to sleep only seven, six, or even five hours a night."[76]

The presence of artificial lights has a profound impact on the physiological systems of our body. Going to bed late at night especially if a person sits in front of computer or television screen (which emit artificial lights) and getting up late in the morning has detrimental effects on a person's health. Allah has installed a natural clock within our bodies (circadian rhythms), which upon the sunset, informs our body to reduce the production of stress hormone, Cortisol, in our body and, instead, increases the production of melatonin, a hormone released in our blood in the darkness of night. Although cortisol has several advantages for our body, its disadvantage is that it speeds up our aging process. It makes us grow old quickly. Conversely, melatonin hormone, which is released by the pineal gland of the brain, not only helps in causing us to sleep but it also aids in doing the construction work in our body.[77] Our bodies are created in such a way that we are meant to get up just before the light of dawn emerges and to go to sleep at nightfall, our hormone levels adjusting to the rise and fall of daylight around us. Now, in our modern world we can fool our hormonal system with artificial lights, which has a big impact on our health. Staying up late with bright artificial lights shining

---

[76] DeNoon, Daniel J. (Feb. 14, 2002) "Are You Sleeping Enough -- or Too Much?" *WebMD Medical News* (Reviewed by Charlotte Grayson Mathis, MD) http://www.webmd.com/sleep-disorders

[77] Beers, Mark H. (2003). *The Merck Manual of Medical Information: Home Edition.* New York, Pocket Books

in our eyes keeps our stress hormone cortisol high when it should be diminishing, and suppresses our sleep hormone melatonin, when it should be rising. This imbalance of cortisol and melatonin in our bodies has an impact on our ability to deal with stress, lose weight, physically and psychologically repair our tissues, feel rested, and be ready for the new day. Consequently, the person's health declines with the passage of time.

Waking up at the time of *tahajjud* also strengthens our mental abilities and improves our brain function. A research was published in 2000 in the *Journal of American College Health*, a highly prestigious medical journal. This survey was conducted on the University students at the Brigham Young University, Utah. In this study, which was performed on 184 first year students of the college, it was concluded that students who habitually go to bed late and sleep late the next day have lower grade point averages (exam scores) than students with early-to-bed and early-to-rise sleeping habits. Out of all the factors studied, weekday and weekend wakeup times had the strongest association with students' grades. Each hour over the average that students slept in on weekdays was associated with a 0.13-point drop on the GPA (Scale of 0 to 4.0). A similar correlation was found for hours spent in bed on weekends, when many students catch up on sleep. This finding tells us that our mental abilities will function better if we fall more in line with natural circadian rhythms, go to sleep earlier and wake up earlier. Commenting on this research, Dr. Joseph Mercola, author of the "Total Health Program" writes: "The reason that this is so important is that our body systems are tied to the natural circadian rhythms of the earth. Our bodies, particularly the adrenal glands, also do most of their healing during the early part of the night."[78]

Human sleep is divided into rapid-eye-movement sleep (REM) and non-REM sleep (NREM), with NREM sleep further sub-divided into stages 1 to 4. Bio-psychologists and sleep-researches assume that the repair of the body takes place during stages 3 and 4 of NREM or dreamless sleep, during which memory and learning molecules are also

---

[78] http://www.mercola.com/2001/jan/14/sleep.htm

re-synthesized in the hippocampus of the brain. From stage 4 of deep sleep, we pass on to stage 5, known as Rapid Eye Movement (REM) sleep, when dreaming occurs. There are 4 or 5 such periods in every night of restful sleep. The dreams of early morning, for example before *Tahajjud* prayers, are remembered more vividly and with more accurate details, compared to the dreams seen the earlier part of the night. This could be because memory molecules are synthesized during stages of deep sleep, which precedes the REM sleep when dreaming occurs. In fact, research has shown that memory enhancement, which happens in the sleep, occurs mostly during the early part of the night.

In one study reported in the 2006 issue of the scientific journal *Nature* (vol. 444) conducted at the University of Lubeck, Germany by Dr. Lisa Marshall and her coworkers, it was found that the consolidation of certain memories occurs during the early part of the night's sleep.[79] In the study, 13 test subjects learned 46 word-pairs in a training session before they went to sleep. Electrodes were then placed on the heads of the sleeping subjects and electrical potentials were applied to their brains to artificially mimic the way human brain consolidates the memory during sleep. Remarkably, the morning after this treatment, the participants in the study demonstrated increased ability to recall the word-pair compared with their performance the morning after receiving a fake treatment. More interesting finding was the timing of stimulation. Dr. Lisa Marshall and her colleagues observed that there was memory enhancement when the stimulation was given in the early part of the night and there was no improvement in memory recall if stimulation was applied during the last part of the night. This means that memory enhancement occurs mostly in the early part of the night and we will not lose anything if we wake up in the later part of the night. It is no wonder that Prophet Muhammad (peace be upon him) preferred to go to sleep early, that is, right after Isha prayer (as narrated in Bukhari) and would wake up in the later portion of the night. Similarly, Umar ibn al-Khattab used to urge people to sleep

---

[79] Marshall, L., Helgadottir, H., Molle, M. & Born, J. (2006) "Boosting slow oscillations during sleep potentiates memory" *Nature* 444, pp. 610-613

early, so that they would not miss the *tahajjud* prayers. To sum up, when a person wakes up in the hours of early dawn and recites the verses of the Qur'an in the *tahajjud* prayers and contemplates on them, the words and the message of the Quranic verses get imprinted on his/her brain and become part of his/her character.

IMPORTANCE OF *TAHAJJUD* FOR PEOPLE DOING DA'WAH WORK

Tahajjud prayers are obligatory on all the Prophets of Allah whereas they are voluntary for the rest of the people. However, *Qiyam Al-Layl* (standing in prayers at night) and getting up for *tahajjud* prayers is extremely important for people who are active in spreading the message of Islam (doing *da'wah* work). There are several reasons for that. People doing the da'wah work are involved in the Prophetic mission about which our Holy Prophet Muhammad (peace be upon him) said: "Indeed, scholars are the inheritors of the Prophets." (Sunan Abu Dawud; Ibn Majah)

When a person engaged in spreading the message of Islam wakes up in the hours of early dawn by sacrificing one's sweet sleep, this causes strengthening of one's will power and faith. Allah says in the Qur'an that *tahajjud* prayers will raise us to a higher status of faith:

"Verily, the rising by night is most effective for controlling the self and most suitable for reciting the Qur'an well." (Surah Al-Muzzammil: 6)

Sleep is a very strong impetus in human beings. In addition, human nature seeks ease and comfort at that time. That is why Allah has said in the Qur'an that it is against the human desires to get up at the time of *tahajjud* for standing in prayers and remembering Allah. This act is an exercise that is most effective in controlling and disciplining the self. The person, who learns self-control over his body by this method, becomes capable of using his power in the way of God, can work more efficiently and firmly to make the message of Islam prevail in the world.

Getting up in the early hours is also an effective method of producing harmony and concord between the heart and the tongue, for during these hours of the night no one else intervenes between the servant and his God, and whatever a person utters with his/her tongue in this state, is the true voice of the person's heart. Moreover, *tahajjud* prayers is a very efficacious means of bringing about conformity between the exterior (dhaahir) and the interior (baatin) of man because a person sacrificing his/her slumber and arising for worship in the depths of the night would do so only out of sincerity. There can be no trace of showing off (riyaa) and hypocrisy in this act.

Since the worship at *tahajjud* is harder on a person than the worship during the daytime, it develops steadfastness in him/her. Such a person can face and endure the hardships in the path of God with greater perseverance and determination. Hence, this form of worship makes it clear who truly loves Allah. A person performing *tahajjud* prayers will most probably not be suffering from the condition of man as mentioned in the famous poem *"Jawab Shikwaa"* (Answer to a Complaint) by the Islamic poet and philosopher, Allama Mohammad Iqbal. In this poem, Allama Iqbal assumed if the Almighty Lord Himself is addressing a complaining Muslim and answering his protest. In one of the poetic verses in his book Bang-e-Dara, Iqbal gives the message of Allah to human beings:

"How difficult for you is waking up at the dawn!
You have no Love for Us, sleep is dear to you"[80]

Renowned Indian Islamic scholar and commentator on the Qur'an, Imam Abul Kalam Azad (died 1968 C.E.) was very fond of waking up in the early hours from his childhood. In his book Ghubaar-e-Khatir (Emotions of the Heart), he states: "One great benefit I got from the habit of early rising is that no one can interrupt in my solitude now. A fire is kindled in my heart in the early hours of dawn and its sparks do not extinguish and keep on working under the ashes.... I am grateful to my father (Sheikh Sadruddin) for instilling in me this habit of early rising. It was his routine that he would always stay awake at the time of *tahajjud*. He would say to us that going to bed early and waking up early is one of the first signs of a successful life."[81]

[80] Iqbal, Sir Mohammad (Allama) (1987). *Bang-e-Dara*. Lahore, Sheikh Ghulam Ali & Sons.
[81] Azad, Maulana Abul Kalaam (1982). *Ghubaar-e-Khatir* (Emotions of the Heart). Lahore, Islamic Publishing House.

Another benefit obtained from the *tahajjud* prayers is that Allah grants his slaves honor and dignity in their personality as mentioned in one *hadeeth* of the Prophet (peace be upon him) narrated by Sahl bin Sa'ad:

> *"Angel Jibreel came to the Prophet of Allah and said: 'O Muhammad! Know that the honor of a Momin (believer) is in offering tahajjud and his respect and greatness (among the people) is in abstinence (from people's riches)."* (Narrated by Tabarani in *Al-Awsat* with a good chain of transmitters)

THE THREE R's – READ, REPENT & RISE

In the Qur'an, Allah has commanded three things to the people involved in spreading the message of Islam in the following three verses:

(1) **Read**

"Read (Iqra)! In the Name of your Lord, Who has created" (Surah Al-'Alaq: 1)

(2) **Repent**

"Rise (Qum il Layl) to pray (and repent) in the night except a little." (Surah Al-Muzzammil: 2

(3) **Rise**

"Arise (Qum fa Andhir) and warn! And your Lord magnify!" (Surah Al-Muddathir: 2, 3)

Interestingly, these verses were the first ones to be revealed to Prophet Muhammad (peace be upon him). Muslim historian and scholar of Qur'anic history, Jalaluddin As-Sayyuti writes in *Al-Itteqan fi Uloom al-Qur'an*: "According to most of the commentators of the Qur'an, the first four surahs (chapters) of the Qur'an revealed to Prophet Muhammad (peace be upon him) were verses from Surah Al-Alaq, Surah Al-Qalam, Surah Al-Muddathir and Surah Al-Muzammil. [82] Those verses provide a recipe of how to make a

---

[82] Sayyuti, Imam Jalaluddin (1982). *Al-Itteqan fi Ulum al-Qur'an.* Lahore, Idara Islaamiyat.

balanced Islamic personality. People who are engaged in spreading the message of Islam must follow those three R's, which are READ, REPENT and RISE (*Iqra, Qum* and *Qum*). The first commandment, Iqra, means that we must seek the knowledge of Islam. *Qum il Layl* implies that we make it a must on ourselves to say *tahajjud* prayers and repent in the early hours to purify ourselves. *Qum fa Andhir* means that we have to rise and convey the message of Islam to other people.

Buiding An Islamic Personality

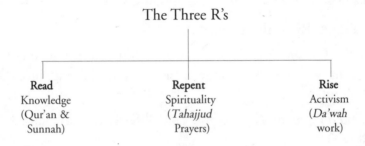

The Three R's

Read	Repent	Rise
Knowledge	Spirituality	Activism
(Qur'an &	(*Tahajjud*	(*Da'wah*
Sunnah)	Prayers)	work)

Hence, a Muslim should be a walking example of Iqra, *Qum* and *Qum*, which can be translated into three concepts, namely, knowledge, spirituality and activism. To act upon only one of those three commandments in the absence of the other two, results in an incomplete Islamic personality. Activism without knowledge and spirituality has no foundations. Knowledge without action is a means without an end. Similarly, knowledge without spirituality, humility and continuous repentance to Allah is a useless entity. *Qiyam al-Layl* is an act of worship that connects one's heart to Allah and enables a person to overcome the temptations of life and to strive against one's own self, at the time when voices are silent, eyes are closed in sleep, and sleepers are comfortably sleeping in their beds. For this reason, *tahajjud* prayers are one of the measures of sincere determination and from the qualities of those who have great ambitions. Such a person will be able to use his knowledge and activism to reform the society around him. In fact, the da'wah workers who have the above mentioned qualities are a great threat for Shaitaan (Satan). Such are the people about whom Shaitaan warned his students in the famous poem by Allama Iqbal titled "Parliament of Iblees" in the following words:

"You will still see some people in this nation here and there. Those who perform ablution with their early morning tears" (Armighan-e-Hijaaz)

In this couplet, Shaitaan warns his disciples that there are still some people present in the Muslim nation who pose a threat for the Satans. These are people who perform ablution with their tears at the time of *tahajjud* prayers. They shed their tears before Allah and ask for His forgiveness and steadfastness in the path of Allah.

MEASURES TO HELP GETTING UP FOR *TAHAJJUD* PRAYERS

Before going to sleep, one should make the intention to perform the *tahajjud* prayers. Abu ad-Darda' quoted the Prophet (peace be upon him) as saying: *"Whoever goes to his bed with the intention of getting up and praying during the night, but, being overcome by sleep, fails to do that, he will have recorded for him what he has intended, and his sleep will be reckoned as a charity (an act of mercy) for him from his Lord."* (an-Nisa'i and Ibn Majah) Overeating before going to bed has to be avoided because it is one of the main barriers that prevent people from getting up for *tahajjud* prayers. When food is digested in the body, alcoholic by-products are generated in the body causing a person to sleep. In addition, too much fatty foods must be avoided especially in the dinner as they may result in coronary heart diseases. According to National Institute of Health, 80% of the diseases in the U.S. are related to food. Excess in eating is the mother of several diseases. Avoiding food and drink too much will make a person light and increase his ability to awaken at night. Sheikh Fatah Mousali, great scholar of Islamic spirituality, once said: "I had the opportunity to sit in the company of 30 of the greatest of Islamic scholars and all of them advised me of the same thing: Avoid too much mixing with people, eat little and talk less."

Strong determination to wake up at the time of *tahajjud* is also necessary. It has been narrated by Abu Huraira that Allah's Apostle said:
*"Satan puts three knots at the back of the head of any of you if he is asleep.
On every knot he reads and exhales the following words, 'The night is long, so
stay asleep.' When one wakes up and remembers Allah, one knot is undone;
and when one performs ablution, the second knot is undone, and when one
prays the third knot is undone and one gets up energetic with a good heart in
the morning; otherwise one gets up lazy and with a mischievous heart."*
(Sahih Bukhari)

Avoiding sins to the best of human ability is extremely important for
someone who wishes to perform the early morning prayers. A person who
commits sins will not be assisted by Allah to pray at night. Therefore,
he/she must be engaged in continual repentance to Allah. Imam Ghazali
in his book *Ihya Uloom ud Din* mentions about the story of an Islamic
scholar who once indulged in backbiting and, as a punishment from
Allah, he kept on missing the *tahajjud* prayers for two full months. [83]

People waste their time at night by sitting in front of television, clicking
on the remote control and changing different TV channels or web surfing on
the Internet. In doing so they may think that they are just killing time. First
of all, the person must realize that we do not kill time. Actually, it is time that
kills us. With every breath, with every tick of the clock, as the time passes, we
get closer to our final destination, to our grave, to our death:

"And that to your Lord (Allah) is the end (Return of everything)."
(Surah An-Najm: 41)

The Prophet (peace be upon him) spoke to us about how much we
lose when we waste our time, saying:

"There are two blessings that many people squander: health and
time." (Sahih Al-Bukhari)

We all know that we will be standing before Allah and questioned
about how we spent our time – Did we spend our time wisely or did we

---

[83] Ghazaali, Imam Abu Hamid (n.d.). *Ihya Uloom ud Din.* Karachi, Darul Isha'at.

just kill it? The Prophet (peace be upon him) said: *"No one will be permitted to turn his two feet away on the Day of Resurrection until he is questioned about four matters: about his life, how he spent it; his youth, how he employed it; his work, what he did with it; and his wealth, how he earned it and spent it."* (At-Tirmidhi) Therefore, unless there is a valid necessity to stay awake until late night (e.g., for students to study for their exams, etc.), we should follow the Prophetic sunnah of going to bed early, after the Isha prayers. When we go to bed late at night, for sure we will have hard time getting up at *tahajjud* prayers. Some Muslims think that waking up for morning prayers is an uphill task for any Muslim but, in reality, if we go to sleep early, we will never have difficulty rising up for the morning prayers, whether that be *tahajjud* or Fajr prayers.

A person has to be determined, consistent and constant with *tahajjud* prayers, even if it is done in small amount, since this was the practice of Prophet Muhammad (peace be upon him) who said in one tradition: *"The most loved deeds to Allah are those which are done consistently, even though they are small."* (Sahih Bukhari & Muslim) Similarly, Abdullah bin Umar narrates that the Prophet (peace be upon him) said to him: "O Abdullah, do not become like so-and-so who used to make the *tahajjud* prayers and then stopped praying it." (Sahih Bukhari & Muslim)

Dr. Joseph Mercola is a medical doctor and author of a new therapeutic program called "Total Health Program." In his method of treating the patients, Dr. Mercola stresses the importance of early-to-bed and early-to-rise. [84] He suggests taking certain measures to help in getting a good night's sleep and waking up early in the morning, which are as follows:

• Sleep in complete darkness or in a room with minimum light in it, such as a night-light. If there is light in the room in which we are sleeping, it can disrupt our circadian rhythm, and it may stop our pineal gland's production of the sleep aid hormone melatonin. Even if we wake up and go to the bathroom in the middle of the night, there should be as little light in the bathroom as possible.

---

[84] Mercola, Joseph "33 Secrets to a Good Night's Sleep (Source: http://www.mercola.com/2001/jan/14/sleep.htm)

• Avoid caffeine before going to bed as it may cause us to lose our sleep.

• Televisions and computers should be kicked out of the bedroom. Their bright lights are too stimulating for the brain, and it will take longer to fall asleep. In addition, it disrupts the production of serotonin and melatonin hormones by the pineal gland in the brain.

• Do not change your bedtime. We should go to bed and wake up at the same times each day, even on the weekends. This helps our body to get into a sleep rhythm and makes it easier to fall asleep and get up early in the morning. Interestingly, Dr. Mercola's advice is in accordance with the idea of the prescribed prayer times in the Islamic teachings. The Qur'an commands Muslims to perform prayers (obligatory as well as optional) at specified times each day (even on the weekends): *"Verily, the prayer (salah) is enjoined on the believers at fixed hours."* (Surah An-Nisa: 103)

• Read something spiritual or religious as this will help to relax. Dr. Mercola advises us not to read anything stimulating, such as a mystery or suspense novel, as this may have opposite effect. Dr. Mercola may not be aware that Muslims are taught by Prophet Muhammad (peace be upon him) to recite portions of the Qur'an including *Ayatul Kursi, Surah al-Falaq, Surah an-Naas, Surah al-Mulk,* before going to sleep. All these measures will help us to get a good quality sleep during the night and wake up early in the morning for *tahajjud* prayers.

SOME TESTIMONIES FROM ISLAMIC HISTORY

If we flip through the pages of Islamic history, we will see that all the Companions of the Prophet and Islamic scholars and pious personalities of later generations were very punctual in performing the *tahajjud* prayers.

Prophet Muhammad (peace be upon him) always had the habit of praying Qiyam Al-Layl, and never gave it up, whether he was traveling or staying at home. It has been narrated by al-Mughira: *"The Prophet used to stand (in the tahajjud prayers) or pray till both his feet or legs swelled. He was asked why (he offered such an unbearable prayer) and he said, 'Should I not be a thankful slave'."* (Sahih Bukhari – Chapter on *Tahajjud*)

All the wives of our Holy Prophet (peace be upon him) used to observe Qiyam al-Layl. Ayesha Siddiqah, the mother of believers, said: *"Do not give up prayer at night, for the Apostle of Allah (peace be upon him) would not leave it. Whenever he fell ill or lethargic, he would offer it sitting."* (Sunan Abu Dawud – Prayer at Night; Book 5, Number 1302) In fact, Anas ibn Malik reported that the Prophet (peace be upon him) said: *"Jibreel said to me, 'Go back to Hafsah (your wife), for she fasts a lot and prays a lot at night (Qiyam Al-Layl).'"* (Al-Hakim)

It has been narrated by Salim's father (Abdullah ibn Umar) that in the lifetime of the Prophet whosoever saw a dream would narrate it to Allah's Apostle. I had a wish of seeing a dream to narrate it to Allah's Apostle (peace be upon him). I was a grown up boy and used to sleep in the Mosque in the lifetime of the Prophet. I saw in the dream that two angels caught hold of me and took me to the Fire which was built all around like a built well and had two poles in it and the people in it were known to me. I started saying, *"I seek refuge with Allah from the Fire."* Then I met another angel who told me not to be afraid. I narrated the dream to Hafsa (my sister) who told it to Allah's Apostle. The Prophet said, *"Abdullah is a good man. I wish he prayed tahajjud."* After that Abdullah ibn Umar (i.e., Salim's father) used to sleep but a little at night. (Sahih Bukhari - Chapter on Prayer at Night)

Sheikh Junaid Baghdadi (died 297 A.H.) was a renowned Islamic scholar. Imam Ghazali in his book Ayyuhal Walad mentions a narration that one Islamic scholar saw Sheikh Junaid Baghdadi in his dream after his death and asked him: "O Abu al-Qasim! Inform me about your state after your death!" Sheikh Junaid Baghdadi responded:

"Worships and deeds all turned out to be useless. The only things that benefited me were some rak`ahs (units) of prayers I used to offer at the time of tahajjud for which Allah forgave me."

Umar bin Abdul Aziz, the celebrated Umayyad Caliph whose empire stretched from the shores of the Atlantic to the highlands of Pamir, is regarded as the fifth Rightly Guided Caliph of the Muslims. His mother, Umme Asim was the grand daughter of Caliph Umar ibn al-Khattab. Despite being the only ruler of the mighty Muslim empire, Umar bin Abdul Aziz would sleep very little at night. He would spend most of his nights in saying prayers and supplicating to Allah for the welfare of the Ummah of Prophet Muhammad (peace be upon him) until it was time for Fajr prayers. What were the effects of the rule of such a God-conscious person on his subjects? According to some historians, Umar's predecessor Caliph Walid bin Abdul Malik loved architecture, and hence, the subjects of his time always used to talk about constructing beautiful buildings. Walid's ruling era was followed by the rule of Suleiman bin Abdul Malik, who loved women and tasty dishes. The people of his time had the beauty of women and delicious dishes on their nerves. When the reign of Caliph Umar bin Abdul Aziz came, the discussion of Islamic teachings became prevalent. When young or old people met each other, they would talk with each other about Qiyam al-Layl and *tahajjud* prayers.

Qutb ud din Bakhtiyar Kaki was a renowned Muslim scholar from Delhi, India, who was one of those responsible for the spread of Islam in the Indian sub-continent. He died on the 14th of Rabiul Awwal, 633 A.H. At the time of his death, he left a will which his student Sheikh Abu Saeed read aloud to people. In his will, Sheikh Kaki made a condition that his funeral prayers should be lead by a person who must have three qualities: (1) He should have never committed any illicit act with any woman, (2) He must have never missed the sunnah prayers before the fard (obligatory) prayers at the time of Asr, and (3) He should have never missed *tahajjud* prayers in his life. According to Allama Manazir Ahsan Ghilaani, there were many scholars and students of knowledge present in the gathering but no one stepped forward to lead the funeral prayers until it was the Asr (late-afternoon prayer) time. Then, a man came forward after crossing the rows of people. He looked at the face of Sheikh Kaki who was in a coffin and addressed him: "My dear Sheikh, I wanted to keep this as a secret but you have disclosed my secret. Why did you do that? If for some reason I could not keep up with those deeds in my later life, how would I show my face to Prophet Muhammad (peace be upon him) on the Day of Judgment?" After saying those words, that man lead the funeral prayers of Sheikh Kaki. The readers may wonder who that man was who never missed his *tahajjud* prayers. Historians tell us that this man was the king of Delhi at that time and the father of the warrior princess Razia Sultana. His name was Sultan Shams-ud-din Altumish.[85]

These few examples tell us how such glittering personalities from Islamic history were committed to worshipping Allah. Today, forget about optional (nawaafil) prayers, many Muslims have even forsaken sunnah prayers. In our times, people spend their whole nights in plays and entertainment. They watch DVDs and video movies, cable and dish TV programs and sports and they waste their night hours web surfing or chatting on the internet without feeling sleepy but the same people start to feel sleepy when they even hear anyone talking about *tahajjud* prayers. If the hearts of people are aware of the sweetness of faith (Imaan), it will become easy for them to wake up in the early hours of dawn to worship Allah just like some people stay awake the whole night to experience the enjoyment of sins. This is a fact that a feeling of emptiness is followed by any pleasure from sins whereas there is a feeling of fulfillment in the heart after a person performs an act of worshipping Allah. And the pleasure obtained from worshipping Allah is much more intense, profound and long-lasting compared to the enjoyment from a sin. Once Hasan Al-Banna advised one of his students in the following words:

"Imaan is a type of sweetness. Try to find it in the act of giving charity and in the two rak`ahs of tahajjud prayers. When you taste this sweetness then Allah will make this as a part of your soul. This is a power when a person gets it, he/she will become steadfast on the path of Allah."

---

[85] Mirathi, Mufti Zainul Aabideen & Akbar-abaadi, Mufti Intizaamullah Shehabi (1991). *Tareekh Millat (History of Muslim Nation)*. (Vol. 3) Lahore, Idara Islamiyat.

CHAPTER SEVEN

Three Optional Monthly Fasts and the Lunar Effects on the Human Body

IN ADDITION TO ONE-MONTH COMPULSORY fasts of Ramadan, Muslims are also encouraged to observe voluntary fasts as those are highly recommended in the traditions of Prophet Muhammad (peace be upon him). Those voluntary fasts include six in the beginning of the month of Shawwal (the lunar month after Ramadan), three in the middle of every lunar month, on the ninth of *Zul-Hajj*, on the ninth or/and tenth of Muharram. As all the commandments of Islam carry a profound wisdom behind them, the observance of voluntary fasts is also beneficial at the individual as well as societal level.

If we ponder over the teachings of the Qur'an and sunnah, we will see that the biggest enemy of human beings is Satan as it is mentioned in the Qur'an:

"Surely, Satan is your open enemy." (Surah Yaseen: 60)

Satan whispers into the hearts of human beings and causes them to go astray from the right path. Fasting is highly effective in our fight against Satan. Prophet Muhammad (peace be upon him) said in a tradition:

"Verily, Satan circulates in the human body as blood does. You should constrict his passages by hunger and fasting." (*Fiqh as-Sunnah*, vol. 3, Sayyid as-Saabiq)

As a digression from the main topic, it may be of interest to the readers to know that people usually think of the English doctor, William

Harvey, to be the one who discovered circulation of blood in the body as it was described in his book *On the Motion of Heart and Blood in Animals* published in 1628 CE. However, the truth is that Prophet Muhammad (peace be upon him) described the motion of blood in human body about 1000 years before William Harvey, as it is clear in the above Prophetic tradition.

In another tradition, Prophet Muhammad (peace be upon him) is noted to have said: *"Fasting is like a shield."* (Musnad Ahmed) It means that fasting is the best form of defense against the onslaughts of our ego-centric self and Satan. For this reason, Prophet Muhammad (peace be upon him) recommended it highly to all Muslims to observe THREE voluntary fasts EVERY month as it is clear in the following traditions:

Abu Dharr al-Ghafari reported:

"The Messenger of Allah ordered us to fast for three days of every month--that is, on the days of the full moon (the 13th, 14th, and 15th of the lunar month). And he said: 'It is like fasting the whole year.'" [86] (an-Nisa'i & Ibn Hibban)

Similarly, in another tradition, Qatadah Ibn Malhan al-Qaysi narrated:

"The Apostle of Allah (peace be upon him) used to command us to fast the days of the white (nights): thirteenth, fourteenth and fifteenth of the month. He said: This is like keeping a perpetual fast." (Sunan Abu Dawud; Kitab As-Saw'm; Number 2443)

In addition, Abdullah ibn Mas'ud reported:

"The Messenger of Allah (peace be upon him) used to fast three days every month." (Sunan Abu Dawud; Kitab As-Saw'm; Number 2444)

In these traditions, Prophet Muhammad (peace be upon him) has specifically commanded Muslims to fast on the 13th, 14th and 15th of the lunar month. What could be the reason for that? That is a good question! Recently, some thought-provoking scientific findings have

---

[86] Ibn Hibban regarded this tradition as sahih [authentic]

110

emerged pertaining to the moon's influence on the human body, particularly during the period of full moon.

Dr. Arnold Leiber (M.D.), Chairman of the Department of Psychiatry at Miami Heart Institute, Florida, did pioneering study at the University of Miami, School of Medicine in the field of the effects of moon on human body. He has summarized his findings as well as myriads of scientific researches done by other scientists pertaining to this subject in his book How the Moon Affects You. Before embarking on this research project, Dr. Leiber made an interesting observation during the onset of his medical career that the rate of occurrences of accidents and disturbed behavior of psychiatric patients increased during the periods of the full moon and then it would go back to normal. In his research project, which was later on published in the 1972 issue of *American Journal of Psychiatry*, Dr. Leiber studied the relevance of murder to the moon cycles in two major cities.[87] He and his collaborator Dr. Carolyn Sherin, a clinical psychologist, statistically analyzed 2,008 murder cases in Cuyahoga County (Cleveland), Ohio from the years 1958 to 1970. Similarly, they analyzed 1,887 murder cases committed in Dade County (Miami), Florida from 1956 to 1970. They were surprised at the results of their studies. Every month, the graphs of homicides showed a striking correlation with the lunar-phase cycle. For a period of about thirteen to fifteen years, it was consistently observed that every month, the most number of murders were committed when it was a full moon. Dr. Leiber later on wrote:

> *"The homicides peaked at full moon!...* Our results indicated that murders became more frequent with this increase in the Moon's gravitational force. The peaks on the graph were significantly greater than could be expected by chance. We had shown statistically that there was a relationship between moon phases and murders."[88]

---

[87] Leiber, A.L. & Sherin, C.R. (1972). "Homicides and the Lunar Cycle: Toward a Theory of Lunar Influence on Human Emotional Disturbances." *American Journal of Psychiatry* 129; 69-74.

[88] Leiber, Arnold L. (M.D.) (1996). *How the Moon Affects You.* New York, Hastings Hous

Similarly, another finding was published in the December 1977 report of National Institute of Mental Heath. The investigating psychologist of that study, Dr. Edward J. Malmstrom of Berkeley's Wright Institute, found statistically significant link between the moon cycles and homicides and suicides that had occurred in Alameda County, California, and in Denver County, Colorado, for the same fifteen-year period (1956 to 1970) as the Dade and Cuyahoga studies.

In the same vein, another scientific study was conducted by two scientists named Jodi Tasso and Elizabeth Miller, of the Department of Psychology, Edgecliff College, in Cincinnati, which was published in the 1976 issue of the Journal of Psychology. It was shown in this paper that the reported incidences of rape, robbery, assault, larceny, auto theft, burglary, drunken behavior and offenses against family were all increased at full moon. [89]

All these scientific studies confirmed the effects of the moon on human behavior. These findings indicate that the lunar cycles have the ability to alter the behavior of many people. In providing the probable underlying cause of those lunar effects, Dr. Leiber noted:

> "Like the surface of the Earth, man is about 80 per cent water and 20 per cent solids. I believe the gravitational force of the Moon, acting in concert with the other major forces of the Universe, exerts an influence on the water in the human body – in you and in me – as it does on the oceans of the planet. Life has, I believe, biological high tides and low tides governed by the Moon. At new and full moon these tides are at their highest – and the Moon's effect on our behavior is its strongest…. Excess body water causes tissue tension, swelling, and nervous irritability. When the Moon's gravitational pull upsets our fluid balance, the result makes us tense and liable to emotional outburst." [90]

---

[89] Tasso, J. & Miller E. (1976). "The Effects of the Full Moon on Human Behavior." *Journal of Psychology* 93 (1); 81-83.
[90] Leiber, Arnold L. (M.D.) (1996). *How the Moon Affects You.* New York, Hastings House.

Hence, when the moon is full, it causes unrest in the behavior of some people who, as a consequence, commit acts of aggression. If we ponder over the last words of Dr. Leiber given above, he is mentioning about excess body water, which is affected by the moon's gravitational pull. When a Muslim fasts on the 13th, 14th and 15th of a lunar month, fasting automatically controls the excess body water. In addition, purpose of fasting is to make the person God-conscious and it is highly unlikely that such a person would commit an act of aggression, for his heart will be pacified by remembrance of Allah because of his fasting. Such a person will not harm the society due to his uncontrolled behavior. Such a person will be a real Muslim – the one totally in submission to Allah. Therefore, we can understand the underlying wisdom in the Prophetic saying regarding voluntary fasting on the three days of full moon.

CHAPTER EIGHT

Contemplating the Qur'an

TODAY, QUR'AN IS THE MOST WIDELY read book but also the least understood book. The majority of Muslims read this book without contemplating on its meanings and message, whether they understand Arabic or not. This book has been underestimated by the majority of them.

Today, Muslims have reduced the Qur'an to a ceremonial book from which they try to attain blessings on special occasions, such as at the time of buying a house, during a marriage ceremony or on the occasion of death of a person. In the words of commentator on the Qur'an, Sheikh Amin Ahsan Islahi, such people are similar to ones who were given cannon to destroy the fortress of Satan but they started to consider it as a mosquito killer machine. Seldom is this Book used to contemplate upon, to do *tadabbur* (contemplate) upon, whereas the companions of Prophet Muhammad (peace be upon him) would perform *tadabbur* on the Qur'an constantly. The companions understood clearly the message of the Qur'an as it is said:

> "*Do they not then think deeply in the Qur'an, or are their hearts locked up (from understanding it)?*" (Surah Muhammad: 24)

Similarly, the Qur'an describes true Muslims as those who "*whenever they are reminded of the revelations of their Lord, do not fling themselves upon them (as if they are) deaf and blind.*" (Surah Al-Furqan: 73). In explaining this verse, Allama Zamakhshari, commentator on the Qur'an, describes those believers as the ones who listen to the Qur'an with wide-awake ears and look into it with seeing eyes. British convert to Islam and former diplomat, Charles Le Gai Eaton sheds light on the subject of contemplation on the Qur'an in the following words in *Islam and the Destiny of Man:*

"The Qur'an holds up a mirror to those who approach it, and if they come to it for the wrong reasons or in the wrong spirit, they will find nothing there. If they are by nature superficial they will find in it only superficialities, and if profound, profundities in corresponding measure."[91]

The purpose of this chapter is to highlight some of the common themes of the Qur'an, which in turn may provide the readers with some of the tools to aide them in doing "*tadabbur*" (contemplation) on the Qur'an when they open it next time. Owing to the vastness of this subject, the author considers this chapter to be a drop in the ocean and only a humble effort on his part to contribute to the subject of contemplation on the Book of the Almighty Allah, about which Prophet Muhammad (peace be upon him) said:

"Repetition does not wear it out and its wonders do not end. It is the Truth. It is not a jest." (At-Tirmidhi)

FOUNDATION OF EVERY CIVILIZATION IS A BOOK

Barry Sanders is an American intellectual and author of the book A is for Ox. In this thought-provoking book, he states that the basis of every civilization is an oral book. Sacred oral traditions are transcribed into that book, which becomes the foundation of a literary civilization.[92] For example, the source of Hindu civilization was the *Vedas*. The starting point of Jewish civilization was the *Torah*. The foundation of Greek civilization was Homer's *Iliad* and *Odyssey*. The origin of Christian civilization was the *Bible*.

Similarly, the basis of Islamic civilization was the *Qur'an*. Before the revelation of the Qur'an, there was no book in Arabic language. Arabs were oral people with brilliant memories. The first book in Arabic language is the Qur'an – "Al-Kitaab" (the Book) as it is rightly said in the Qur'an itself:

---

[91] Eaton, Charles Le Gai (1985). *Islam and the Destiny of Man*. New York, The Islamic Texts Society.
[92] Sanders, Barry (1995). *A is for ox*. New York, Vintage Books.

"This is the Book; in it is guidance sure, without doubt." (Surah Al-Baqarah: 2)

Before Islam, the Arabs were a nation of Ummiyeen (illiterate people) and yet this Book laid the foundations of the most literary civilization the world had ever seen. At one point, no nation on the face of this planet could compete with the Islamic libraries in Baghdad and Qurtuba (Cordova of Muslim Spain). This was all due to the strength of the Qur'an as it is mentioned in a Prophetic tradition:

> *"Indeed, Allah will uplift many nations because of this Book (Qur'an) and debase many nations because of it."* (Sahih Muslim, narrated by Na'fi)

In his book Art of Islam: Language and Meaning, German-Swiss philosopher, Titus Burckhardt, explains the impact of Qur'an on Arab civilization as follows:

> *"In Arabic, the 'tree' of verbal forms, of derivatizations from certain roots, is quite inexhaustible; it can always bring forth new leaves, new expressions to represent hitherto dormant variations of the basic idea – or action. This explains why this Bedouin tongue was able to become the linguistic vehicle of an entire civilization very rich and differentiated."*[93]

Titus' observation about the language of the Qur'an is very true. In fact, the revelation of the Qur'an in Arabic language itself is no less than a miracle as the Qur'an declares:

> *"Surely, We have sent it down as an Arabic Qur'an, in order that you may learn wisdom."* (Surah Yusuf: 2)

Qur'an turned Arabic language into an international language and Islamic civilization into a universal civilization. According to the classification of the UNO, there are 3000 languages in this world today. Out of these, only 78 are in written form. Out of these, only 8 are universally

---

[93] Burckhardt, Titus (1976). *Art of slam: Language and Meaning*. London, Islamic Festival Trust Ltd.

used. They have their literature universally read and Arabic language is one of those 8 universal languages. Qur'an took a nation of illiterates and made them one of the most literate nations of the world. Malik Bennabi, renowned Algerian Muslim thinker and social scientist, notes in his book The Quranic Phenomenon that the Arabs before Islam loved and admired the eloquence in Arabic language more even so than they loved idols which they worshipped. No wonder when the Qur'an was revealed to them with its miraculous Arabic language, those people fell in love with this Book and began to lead their lives by the commandments of that Book.[94] According to Bennabi, one of the reasons for the decline of Muslims today is that they have forsaken the Qur'an, which is largely due to their ignorance of the Quranic Arabic. This applies not only to the non-Arabs but to the Arabs as well who have also become negligent of the eloquent Quranic Arabic.

History tells us that the eloquence of the Quranic Arabic mesmerized both Muslims and non-Muslims at one point. 'Umar bin al-Khattab himself, who was one of the few educated Arabs, was converted under the effect of this charm, while al-Walid bin al-Mughirah, who personified the eloquence of the literary pride of his period, expressed his opinion concerning the "magic of the Qur'an." Answering Abu Jahl who asked him about his opinion of it, he said: "What do I think of it? By God, I think there is nothing of its like... it is too majestic to be matched!" (*Sirah Ibn Hishaam*) Once Jubayr ibn Mut'im, a polytheist from Makkah who had not embraced Islam yet, came to visit Medina and he said, "I heard the Prophet (peace be upon him) reciting *Surah at-Tur* in the Maghrib prayer. When he reached the Quranic verse, *'Or were they created out of nothing, or are they the creators? Or did they create the heavens and the earth? No, in truth they have no certainty. Or do they possess the treasuries of your Lord or do they have control of them?'* (Surah At-Tur: 35-37) My heart practically flew to Islam." (Sahih Al-Bukhari) Eminent English intellectual and convert to Islam, Mohammad

[94] Bennabi, Malik (2001). *The Quranic Phenomenon: An Essay of a Theory on the Qur'an.* Kuala Lumpur, Islamic Book Trust.

Marmaduke Picktall, in his famous English translation of the Holy Qur'an described the Qur'an as "the inimitable symphony, the very sound of which moves men to tears and ecstasy."[95] In praising the beautiful rhythm and rhetoric of the Qur'an, Professor A.J. Arberry, another British intellectual and historian wrote in his translation of the Qur'an:

> *"In making the present attempt... to produce something which might be accepted as echoing however faintly the sublime rhetoric of the Arabic Koran, I have been at pains to study the intricate and richly varied rhythms which-apart from the message itself-constitute the Koran's undeniable claim to rank amongst the greatest literary masterpieces of mankind."*[96]

Scottish scholar of Middle Eastern history and Islam, H.A.R. Gibb, described in his book *Arabic Literature. An introduction the influence of the Qur'an on the Arabic literature* in the following words:

> "The influence of the Koran on the development of Arabic Literature has been incalculable, and exerted in many directions. Its ideas, its language, its rhymes pervade all subsequent literary works in greater or lesser measure."[97]

Imam Shaafi understood the importance of this hundreds of years ago when he emphasized the importance of learning Arabic in his book on Islamic jurisprudence titled *Ar-Risala* as follows:

> "It is obligatory (*wajib*) on every Muslim (male and female) to learn Arabic language to their capacity."

IMPORTANCE OF STORIES IN THE QUR'AN

If we look at the style of Qur'an, we will notice that one of the ways

---

[95] Pickthall, Mohammad Marmaduke (1996). *The Meaning of the Glorious Qur'an: Text & Explanatory Translation* (ed. By Arafat K. El Ashi). Maryland, Amana Publications.
[96] Arberry, Arthur John (1996). *The Qur'an Interpreted: A Translation* New York, Touchstone.
[97] Gibb, H.A.R. (1963). *Arabic Literature. An introduction.* UK, Clarendon Press.

the Qur'an presents its message to the mankind is through narration of real stories. Qur'an mentions about the narratives of previous nations. Qur'an also talks about parables. One reason is that a story can convey a message in such a simple form that may be hard to convey in the form of dry exposition. Another reason is that story is a part of history. The Qur'an tells us to learn from history. In Qur'an, Allah (the Most Exalted One) says:

"So relate the stories, perhaps they may reflect."(Surah Al-A'raf: 176)

Barry Sanders notes in his book *A is for Ox* that the most characteristic feature of the oral book, which is the basis of any civilization, is that it contains stories and narratives. "Stories are the lifeblood of oral cultures," writes Sanders, and those stories contain everything – "history, truth, heroism, religion, philosophy, morality, love."[98] Many psycholinguists consider that a profound relationship exists between the process of living itself and narrating a story. According to the psychologist Jerome Bruner, narration is linked to self-consciousness itself because every person's life in itself is a story, which he or she carries in his/her memory and reinterpret and recall throughout their lives.[99] Hence, every person's life is a narrative of a series of events linked into an intricate narrative pattern. Therefore, people take interest in narratives and love to hear stories.

Books such as Vedas, Torah, Iliad, Odyssey, and Bible all contain stories. Similarly, the Qur'an also contains stories. In addition, the stories of the Qur'an are all true and free from any human interpolation unlike other religious books. In fact, the Qur'an is the "best of the narratives" as it is said in Surah Yusuf:

"We narrate to you the best of narratives, by Our revealing to you this Qur'an, though before this you were certainly one of those who did

---

[98] Sanders, Barry (1995). *A is for ox.* New York, Vintage Books.
[99] Bruner, Jerome and Susan Weisser (1982). *Literacy and Orality.* (editors David R. Olson & Nancy Torrance) Cambridge, Cambridge University Press, pp. 129 -130.

not know." (Surah Yusuf: 3)

The Qur'an narrates many stories from which deep meanings emerge, to guide the humanity. This is in accordance with human nature. The desire to hear narratives is ingrained and enshrined in human personality and the Qur'an is well aware of that. In another place, the Qur'an tells us:

"And all that We relate to you (O Muhammad peace be upon him) of the stories of the Messengers is in order that We may make strong and firm your heart thereby. And in this has come to you the truth, as well as an admonition and a reminder for the believers." (Surah Hud: 120)

Commenting on the theme of narrative in the Qur'an, Mohammad Asad, Austrian convert and commentator on the Qur'an, writes in his commentary The Message of the Qur'an:

"It cannot be stressed too often that 'narrative' as such is never the purpose of the Qur'an; whenever it relates the stories of earlier prophets, or alludes to ancient legends or to historical events that took place before the advent of Islam or during the lifetime of the Prophet, the aim is invariably a moral lesson; and since one and the same event, or even legend, usually has many facets revealing as many moral implications, the Qur'an reverts again and again to the same stories, but every time with a slight variation of stress on this or that aspect of the fundamental truths underlying the Quranic revelation as a whole...." At another place, he further states that in the Qur'an, the "many-sided, many-layered truth" underlying these stories invariably has a bearing "on some of the hidden depths and conflicts within our own human psyche."[100]

As pointed out above, repetition is another style of the Qur'an, the pur-

---

[100] Asad, Mohammad (2003). *The Message of the Qur'an.* Watsonville (California), The Book Foundation.

pose of which is to incite the reader to contemplate (do *tadabbur*) on the message of the Qur'an. The Qur'an itself attests to this at various places:

> *"And certainly We have repeated (warnings) in this Qur'an that they may be mindful."* (Surah Al-Isra: 41)

> *"Thus do We repeat the Ayaat (proofs, evidences, lessons, signs, revelations, etc.) for a people who give thanks."* (Surah Al-A'raf: 58)

> *"See how We repeat the Ayaat that they may understand."* (Surah Al-An'am:65)

Every repetition in the Qur'an serves a beneficial purpose, either offering more details or putting forward specific moral values to learn. One of the names of the Qur'an is 'Adh-Dhikr', which means, 'the Reminder'. The reminder is repeated in various ways so that the moral value it teaches remains present and alive in the believer's heart and mind. The message is reinforced in the mind of the reader. Every instance of repetition in the Qur'an uses the most eloquent Arabic speech and different ways to describe the same meaning. Repetition strengthens a person's experience in orality because, as Barry Sanders puts it: "Repetition casts a powerful spell in orality." This is important because "a rich experience of orality is an indispensable prelude to literacy."[101]

One way to express diverse meanings in repetition is to have poetic rhythm as Sanders notes: "The rhythm provides a pleasurable and reassuring repetition, like a heart beat, so that the meaning, riding on top of it, can change slightly – and advance the action – over the course of the narrative."[102] Another attribute of the Qur'an, which adds to its beauty, is its poetic rhythm. With its repetition and mesmerizing poetic rhythm, the message of the Qur'an is reinforced into the minds of its readers and at the same time, they learn new morals and new meanings. After all, Prophet Muhammad (peace be upon him) testified about the Qur'an:

---

[101] Sanders, Barry (1995). *A is for ox.* New York, Vintage Books.
[102] Ibid.

"Repetition does not wear it out and its wonders do not end." (At-Tirmidhi)

THEME OF OPPOSITES IN THE QUR'AN

One of the subsidiary names given to the Qur'an is Al-Furqaan, which is translated as "The Discrimination" or "The Criterion." Thus, Qur'an acts as a "sword of discrimination", which cuts through the confusion in human mind between truth and falsehood and between good and evil. There is a proverb in the Arabic language that says: "Things are recognized by their opposites." Indeed, the Qur'an acts as a criterion by which the opposites can be recognized. Professor Toshihiko Izutsu of the Keio University (Tokyo) was a renowned Japanese philosopher who died recently. His genius can be recognized by the fact that he knew more than 30 languages of the world. Needless to say, he was an expert in the Arabic language. In fact, he wrote a book after his many years research on the Qur'an titled *Ethico-Religious Concepts in the Qur'an.* In this book, Professor Izutsu mentioned that in the Qur'an (unlike other religious scriptures) the "theme of opposites" and their comparison are very common. In the Qur'anic worldview, there is a dynamic interplay of opposites in the existence of this world as Professor Izutsu observes:

> "The Quranic outlook divides all human qualities into two radically opposed categories.... In fact, throughout the Qur'an there runs the keynote of dualism regarding the moral values of man: the basic dualism of believer and unbeliever. In this sense, the ethical system of Islam is of a very simple structure. For by the ultimate yardstick of 'belief' one can easily decide to which of the two categories a given person or a given act belongs."[103]

The "basic dichotomy of moral properties" to which Professor Izutsu is referring appears in the Quranic verses in a number of different forms. For example, it may appear in the form of an essential opposition of

---

[103] Izutsu, Toshihiko (2002). *Ethico-Religious Concepts in the Qur'an.* Montreal, McGill-Queen's University Press.

kaafir (disbeliever) and mu'min (believer):

"It is He who created you. But one of you is a kaafir, and one of you is a mu'min. Allah sees everything you do." (Surah At-Taghabun: 2) Or it may emerge in the form of an opposition of muslim (he who has surrendered) and mujrim (sinful):

"Shall We treat the muslimin in the same way as the mujrimin?" (Surah Al-Qalam: 35)

Or that basic dichotomy could be seen between the 'Fellows of the Right' or 'the Dwellers of Paradise' and 'the Fellows of the Left' or 'the Dwellers of Hell' as described in the Qur'an:

"Not equal are the dwellers of the Fire and the dwellers of the Paradise. It is the dwellers of Paradise that will be successful." (Surah Al-Hashr: 20)

Professor Izutsu's observation about the Quranic theme of opposites is very insightful. The Qur'an informs us about the two paths:

"There is no compulsion in religion. Verily, the Right Path has become distinct from the wrong path." (Surah Al-Baqarah: 256)

Hence, for a person who is interested in contemplating (doing *tadabbur*) on the Qur'an, this concept of the theme of opposites will help them in understanding the Qur'an. The person contemplating on the Qur'an will see that it is like a spiritual light that brings out all potential contrasts. He/she will see in the Qur'an the struggle and conflict between faith and infidelity or between those who were true to this commitment and those who betrayed it. The most often narrated story of Prophet Musa [Moses] (peace be upon him) and Pharaoh, the King of Egypt is in reality a perpetual struggle between the followers of Allah and the followers of Satan respectively. Thus, the Qur'an shows both ways to the person and leaves it upon his/her discretion which to choose:

"And (have We not) shown him the two ways (good and evil)?"
(Surah Al-Balad: 10)

QUESTIONING-STYLE OF THE QUR'AN

Another style of the Qur'an is to ask questions to its readers. Usually, the attention spans of people are limited while reading any book. The Qur'an continuously questions people about their beliefs, origin, death and afterlife, deeds, etc. In doing so, the Qur'an not only makes its reader think, but also keeps them attentive, because, after all, those questions are pertaining to our very nature. In addition, the questions asked by the Qur'an are very reflective and make everyone, whether young or old, educated or layman, to ponder over the purpose of their life on this earth. Furthermore, the Qur'an not only asks questions but also provides answers for those inquisitive minds in search of a truth. The questions asked in the Qur'an are, for example:

"Then where are you going?" (Surah At-Takwir: 26

"Then in what statement after this (the Qur'an) will they believe?"
(Surah al-Mursalaat: 50)

"Do they not then think deeply in the Qur'an, or are their hearts locked up (from understanding it)?" (Surah Muhammad: 24)

"Tell Me! The water that you drink. Is it you who cause it from the rain clouds to come down, or are We the Causer of it to come down?"
(Surah Al-Waqiah: 68, 69)

Commenting on the questioning-style of the Qur'an, Western Muslim convert, Sheikh Hamza Yusuf Hanson notes:

"The Qur'an demands that you question things. There are constant rhetorical questions in it: Where then are you going?

---

[104] Barboza, Steven (1993). *American Jihad: Islam After Malcolm X.* New York, Doubleday Dell Publishing Group.

What speech are you going to believe in after this if not the Qur'an? Abraham says, Do you worship what you make with your hands? And we can apply that to the consumer society." [104]

Qur'an – The Book of Advice and Guidance

The Qur'an is the Word of Allah that was revealed to Prophet Muhammad (peace be upon him) over a period of 23 years. It is a book of guidance and good advice:

> *"O mankind! There has come to you a good advice from your Lord (i.e., the Qur'an), and a healing for that (disease) in your breasts - a guidance and a mercy for the believers."* (Surah Yunus: 57)

The Qur'an is different from other books in the sense that when someone looks superficially at the Qur'an, he/she may mistakenly notice incoherence in the Qur'an (although this is NOT the case as it will be shown later in this chapter). However, this is the miracle of the Qur'an that whatever page we open it from, there is guidance for us. British Muslim convert, Charles Gai Eaton comments about this quality of Qur'an in his book Islam and the Destiny of Man:

> "The Qur'an provides a rope of salvation for people of every kind, the stupid as well as the intelligent, and limited interpretations do not diminish its efficacy, provided they satisfy the needs of particular souls. No book of human authorship can be 'for everyone', but this is precisely the function of a revealed scripture, and for this reason it cannot be read in the way that works of human origin are read. The sun and the moon are for everyone – the rain too – but their action in relation to each individual is different and ultimately, to some they bring life and to some death. It could be said that the Qur'an is 'like' these natural phenomenon…" [105]

---

[105] Eaton, Charles Le Gai (1985). *Islam and the Destiny of Man*. New York, The Islamic Texts Society.

The Qur'an, unlike other books of Islamic jurisprudence, is not a book comprised of only commandments. In fact, out of the 6,236 verses of the Qur'an, only about 600 pertain to legal commandments (ahkaam). The remaining portion of the Qur'an discusses subjects such as death, life hereafter and stories of previous prophets and nations in order to admonish and provide spiritual training (tarbiyyah) to Muslims. After all, how a book containing only legal rules about permissible and forbidden (halal and haram) be sufficient for human beings to fight off their most dangerous enemy Shaitaan or Satan (especially when humans cannot even see their enemy). Sheikh Amin Ahsan Islaahi, renowned commentator on the Qur'an, sheds light on this aspect of the Qur'an in his book *Mubaadi Tadabburul Qur'an*:

> "In the Qur'an, commandments and rules are not presented in the way they are presented in books of Islamic law (fiqh). In the Qur'an, before and after every command and law, the attributes of Allah and the Life Hereafter are reminded repeatedly and the spiritual, social, and moral benefits of Allah's commandments are expounded in such a way that touches the human heart. If you read any book of Islamic law (fiqh), you heart will remain unaffected by it but if you read the same commandments in the Qur'an, the part of your soul will be enlightened by its greatness and you will be moved to act upon those commands."[106]

COHERENCE (*NAZM*) IN THE QUR'AN

Another aspect of the Qur'an, the knowledge of which can make *tadabbur* on the Qur'an an exciting experience, is the presence of structural and thematic coherence (*nazm*) in the whole Qur'an. Allah says in the Qur'an:

"So I swear by the position of "an-nujuum." And verily, that is indeed a great oath, if you but know. That (this) is indeed an honorable recital (the Noble Qur'an)." (Surah Al-Waaqiah: 75-77)

[106] Islaahi, Sheikh Ameen Ahsan (1999). *Mubaadi Tadabburul Qur'an*. Lahore, Faraan Foundation.

An-Nujuum in the Arabic language not only means stars, but it also means verses of the Qur'an. According to Ibn Kathir, *mawaaqih an-nujuum* means steady revelation of the Qur'an. (Tafseer Ibn Kathir) Imam Raaghib al-Isfahaani writes in his *Mufridaatul Qur'an* (Dictionary of the Qur'an) that one of the meanings of An-Nujuum is "verses of the Qur'an." There appears to be a degree of similarity between the stars in the heaven and the verses in the Qur'an. Similarly, while explaining the above-mentioned verses of Surah Al-Waaqiah, Imam Abul Kalam Azad, an eminent commentator on the Qur'an, wrote the following in his *Tafseer Tarjumanul Qur'an*:

> *"To take an oath of the 'position of the stars' for the honorable Qur'an means that just as the stars in the universe are present in a highly coherent system, this Qur'an and its verses are also arranged in a highly coherent arrangement."* [107]

With a superficial look, the stars in the heaven may appear disorganized, but in reality there is a great exactness in their positions as modern astronomy tells us. Similarly, there is tremendous exactness and coherence or *nazm* in the way the verses of the Qur'an are organized.

Very few commentators on the Qur'an wrote on this subject owing to the vastness of this subject. In addition, since knowledge of nazm at various places in the Qur'an is based on human understanding, there is a difference of opinion in the way different commentators understood that nazm in the Qur'an. The first person who touched on the subject of nazm in the Qur'an was the Muslim linguist and semanticist Abdul Qahir al-Jurjaani (died 1078 CE). Then, Jalal ud Din As-Suyyuti and Imam Fakr ud Din ar-Razi wrote on this topic. In the twentieth century, the late Indian Islamic scholar and commentator Hameed uddin Farahi (d. 1930 CE) concentrated on this subject, and his famous student Sheikh Amin Ahsan Islahi explained it and carried it further in his multi-voluminous

---

[107] Azad, Maulana Abul Kalaam (1931). *Tafseer Tarjumanul Qur'an.* Vol 3. Lahore, Islamic Academy.

commentary on the Qur'an titled *Tadabbarul Qur'an*. What is nazm in the Qur'an? Sheikh Islahi defines it as follows:

> "*Nazm* means that every chapter (surah) of the Qur'an has a distinct theme and all the verses (ayaat) of that chapter revolve around that central theme. After repeatedly reciting the same chapter of the Qur'an, its central theme becomes obvious and then, the whole chapter appears as a distinct unit instead of a collection of verses on various subjects. It is important to appreciate this nazm in order to understand the Qur'an." [108]

Some aspects of *nazm* may include wisdom in naming different chapters of the Qur'an and their relationship to the verses found in those respective chapters or it may be found in the sequence in which different things are described within various verses of the Qur'an or the way things and their opposites are described together. The following are some of the examples of nazm in the Qur'an with the hope that they may give a direction to people doing *tadabbur* on the Qur'an to explore this vast field in the Qur'an:

1. In Surah Ar-Rehman, while describing the creation, human beings are mentioned before the jinns:

> "*He created man (Adam) from sounding clay like the clay of pottery. And the jinns did He create from a smokeless flame of fire.*" (Surah Ar-Rehman: 14, 15)

On the other hand, later in the same Chapter of the Qur'an, when the challenge to pass beyond the boundaries of the heavens is given, the jinn are addressed before the humans:

> "*O assembly of jinns and men! If you have power to pass beyond the zones of the heavens and the earth, then pass (them)! But you will never be able to pass them, except with authority (from Allah)!*" (Surah Ar-Rehman: 33)

---

[108] Islaahi, Sheikh Ameen Ahsan (1999). *Mubaadi Tadabburul Qur'an*. Lahore, Faraan Foundation.

Why is it so? This is so because human beings are superior to the jinns in terms of creation. Humans are regarded as the best of creation in the Qur'an. However, in terms of traveling huge distances in this universe, jinns are far more superior to humans. Therefore, in the second verse, jinns are challenged before the humans.

2. Both fornication and hypocrisy are signs of a diseased heart. Prophet Muhammad (peace be upon him) said in a tradition: "The fornicator is not a believer while he commits fornication." (Bukhari, Muslim) When we look in the Qur'an, we will notice that fornication and hypocrisy appear together. In Surah An-Noor (The Light), when the punishment of fornication and the rulings concerning Islamic dress are mentioned, right after these verses the traits of hypocrisy and the hypocrites are described. Similarly, in Surah Al-Ahzaab, along with the rulings of hijaab (covering), the subject of hypocrites is also discussed. This *nazm* of the Qur'an shows that there exists a relationship between fornication and hypocrisy.

3. In the Qur'an, wherever *salah* (prayers) is mentioned, almost always *zakah* (obligatory charity) is mentioned along with it. This shows that the two are related to each other and if we negate one of them, the other is also nullified. In fact, the first rightly guided caliph Abu Bakr Siddique used the evidence from the nazm of the Qur'an when he declared those tribes to be apostates who refused to pay *zakah* to the Caliph. *Salah* and *zakah* always appear together in the Qur'an and it was already clear to all of the companions that any Muslim who considers prayers nullified is considered an apostate.[109]

4. Islam is a religion of nature. Muslims are made a middle nation. Our Prophet Muhammad (peace be upon him) loved the color green because it is a middle color. In the spectrum of 7 colors of a rainbow, the green color appears exactly in the middle (i.e., violet, indigo, blue, GREEN, yellow, orange, red). The Qur'an tells us that the Muslim nation is a justly balanced nation:

[109] Faraahi, Imam Hameed uddin (1999). *Rules of Tafseerul Qur'an*. Lahore, Idara Tadabburul Qur'an & *Hadeeth*.

"Thus We have made you a justly balanced nation, that you be witnesses over mankind and the Messenger (Muhammad peace be upon him) be a witness over you." (Surah Al-Baqarah: verse no. 143)

Interestingly, Surah Al-Baqarah has a total of 246 verses. The middle of 246 is 143 and this is exactly where this verse (number 143) appears in Surah Al-Baqarah. Hence, the nazm in the verses of the Qur'an is an aspect of *ijazul Qur'an* (the miraculous nature of the Qur'an).

HOW TO PREPARE YOURSELF TO DO *TADABBUR* ON THE QUR'AN?

The first step towards doing *tadabbur* on the Qur'an is to make the right intention. The purpose of reflecting on the Qur'an is to search for truth and guidance. The purpose of opening the Book and reciting is not to do mere research or to do a mental exercise. Instead, the intention of doing *tadabbur* on the Qur'an is to ponder over the message of the Qur'an and then implement what we learn from the Qur'an on our character and in our life. The Qur'an is a pragmatic book. It is a book of action and not for philosophical hairsplitting. It is guidance for those who would like to act on it:

"These are verses of the Book of Wisdom. A guidance and a mercy for the doers of goodness." (Surah Luqman: 2, 3)

Another extremely important prerequisite for doing *tadabbur* on the Qur'an is to be God-conscious because the Qur'an tells us:

"This is the Book; in it is guidance sure, without doubt, to those who fear Allah." (Surah al-Baqarah: 2)

One must NOT approach the Qur'an with preconceived ideas in the mind, trying to understand the Qur'an through his/her own lens. Instead, one must read the Qur'an with the desire and intention to seek guidance from this Divine Message. The Qur'an clarifies that there are two types of verses in it:

"In it (the Qur'an), there are Verses that are entirely clear, they are the

131

foundations of the Book (known as al-Muhkamaat); and others not entirely clear (al-Mutashabihaat). So as for those in whose hearts there is a deviation (from the truth) they follow that which is not entirely clear thereof, seeking to mislead and seeking for its hidden meanings, but none knows its hidden meanings except Allah. And those who are firmly grounded in knowledge say: "We believe in it; the whole of it (clear and unclear Verses) are from our Lord." And none receive admonition except men of understanding." (Surah Ale-Imran: 7)

In the same vein, the Qur'an classifies its readers into two categories as well: those who are firmly grounded in knowledge and those with a deviation in their hearts. The second category of people tries to mould the meanings of the Qur'an in accordance with their own desires. Such people can cite scripture for their own purpose, as many deviant sects throughout the history of Islam tried to prove their deviant ideologies by misinterpreting or misquoting the Qur'an. Such people do not gain any benefit from the Qur'an because they believe in one part of the Qur'an while they disregard the other part of the Qur'an. On the other hand, people who gain actual benefit from doing *tadabbur* on the Qur'an are the ones who are firmly grounded in their knowledge. They build their knowledge upon the understanding of al-Muhkamaat (clear verses of the Qur'an) and the authentic sunnah of the Prophet (peace be upon him). Such people of understanding approach the Qur'an with the right intention and mind and they reap its fruits in this world as well as the Next World.

HOW DID THE PROPHETIC COMPANIONS *DO TADABBUR* ON THE QUR'AN?

The companions (*sahaabah*) of the Prophet (peace be upon him) were the first group of people who were addressed by the Qur'an. They used to do *tadabbur* on the Qur'an and, in addition, they used to arrange for collective Quranic lectures (*daroos*) in which the Qur'an was explained. The companions of the Prophet (peace be upon him) had established circles in which people would gather and do collective contemplation on the message of the Qur'an. Prophet Muhammad (peace be upon him) encouraged people to establish and join such circles. It is narrated in one *hadeeth* of Prophet Muhammad (peace be upon him):

> *"When a group of people gather in a house, reciting the Book of Allah and studying it between them, tranquility will descend upon them, mercy will befall them, the Angels will encircle them, and Allah will mention them to those who are with Him (i.e., the Angels)."* (Sunan Abu Dawud – Kitaabul Witr)

This prophetic tradition not only tells us that Quranic study circles are blessed but it also tells us that at the time of Prophet Muhammad (peace be upon him), this method of studying the Qur'an was very popular. At that time, the Companions used to participate in such meetings where they would contemplate on the verses of the Qur'an. Prophet Muhammad (peace be upon him) himself participated in such gatherings to such an extent that it has been narrated in some traditions that he preferred the circles doing *tadabbur* on the Qur'an over the circles doing zikr and worship alone. He went and sat in the Quranic study circle and said that he has been sent as a teacher. Some of the narrations tell us that after the Prophet (peace be upon him), the Rightly Guided Caliphs, especially Umar bin Khattab, always took interest in such Quranic study circles that would do *tadabbur* on the Qur'an.

The Companions of the Prophet (peace be upon him) used to do so much *tadabbur* on the Qur'an that Islamic history could not reproduce the examples of their likes. It has been narrated in Muwatta of Imam Malik: "Abdullah bin Umar did *tadabbur* on Surah Al-Baqarah for eight continuous years." The Companions used to contemplate on the Qur'an deeply and then they would make the fruit of their contemplation to be part of their character and action.

When Muslims in a society start to make the Qur'an as the focal point of their attention and start to do *tadabbur* on the Qur'an individually and collectively, this has long lasting effects on the society. The conscience of the society at the time of Prophet Muhammad (peace be upon him) was raised precisely due to their deep attachment with the Qur'an.

The same effect was seen at various points in Islamic history. For example, Farhat Abbas in his book entitled, *The Night of Imperialism*, says, "The social awakening of countries of North Arica, namely Morocco, Algeria and Tunisia began the day when Sheikh Mohammad Abduh went to North Africa and began teaching the interpretation of the Qur'an, a subject that had not customarily been taught in the circles of religious learning." We can see here that although the author of this book himself was not religious, he still recognized that the awakening and changes in North African countries began when the Muslims of those countries started to do *tadabbur* on the Qur'an and organized and established Quranic study circles. This effect of the Qur'an to bring social awakening at a grand scale should not be surprising as the Prophet Muhammad (peace be upon him) said about this Qur'an: *"Indeed, Allah will uplift many nations because of this Book (Qur'an) and debase many nations because of it."* (Sahih Muslim, narrated by Na'fi)

CONCLUSION

The purpose of this chapter is to encourage *tadabbur* on the Qur'an and provide themes to the readers in order to give them a head start in their individual and collective contemplation of the Qur'an. We all need to understand and apply the Qur'an to our lives. We should not reduce the Qur'an to be merely a ceremonial book, i.e., to use the Qur'an on special occasions for attaining blessings. Instead, the Qur'an should serve as the lighthouse for our journey towards Allah. The companions of the Prophet Muhammad (peace be upon him) used to apply every verse of the Qur'an towards their character. We must remember that the Qur'an cures the rust of our hearts when we do *tadabbur* on it. Prophet Muhammad (peace be upon him) said in one narration:

> *"Undoubtedly, the heart gets rusted like metal gets rusted when water goes over it. The People asked, 'How can they [hearts] be cleaned.' The Prophet replied, 'To remember death in abundance and to recite the Holy Qur'an.'"* (Narrated by Abdullah bin Umar in Al-Bayhaqi & At-Tirmidhi)

CHAPTER NINE

The Concept of Afterlife in Islam

THE EPHEMERAL NATURE OF THIS worldly life necessitates the existence of an Afterlife. Allah is Just and manifests His justice. He has established the system of accountability. Those who do good deeds will be rewarded and those who do wrong actions will be punished accordingly. Thus, He created Heaven and Hell and there are admission criteria for both. Muslims believe that the present life is a temporary one. It is a test and if we pass the test, we will be given a life of permanent pleasure in the company of good people in Heaven.

The belief in the Next Life or the Day of Reckoning is extremely important because without such a belief, it is difficult for human beings to obey any moral teachings and values. There is no sense of accountability for our hidden actions, for example. Atheism eventually leads to negation of morality precisely for this reason. When there is no religion, there is no concept of Afterlife and, as a consequence, no concept of moral value. In fact, German atheist philosopher Nietzsche considered human morality and conscience an obstacle in his preaching of atheism. He wrote in his book *Thus Spoke Zarathustra*: "Get rid of the conscience, compassion, forgiveness – those inner human tyrants. Oppress the weak, climb over their corpses..." [110] It is so because morality is accentuated in religion but atheism is against religion. In describing the nature of morality, Muslim intellectual Alija Ali Izetbegovic notes the following in his book *Islam between East and West*:

> *"Morality was born by prohibition and has remained a prohibition until today. A prohibition is religious by nature and by origin. Out*

---

[110] Nietzsche, Friedrich (1995). *Thus Spoke Zarathustra: A Book for All and None*. New York, Modern Library.

of the Ten Commandments, eight of them are prohibitions. Morality is always a restrictive or prohibitive principle which opposes the animal instincts in human nature." [111]

Hence, the implications of having a belief in the Afterlife go beyond just having a belief. The belief in the Afterlife is manifested in the actions of those individuals who are the bearers of that belief. Unfortunately, one of the ways people engage in the denial of death is by disbelieving in the concept of the life in the Hereafter. Qur'an tells us about the disbelievers of the afterlife

"He says: "Who will give life to these bones when they have rotted away and became dust?" (Surah Yaseen: 78)

Today, with the advent of cloning, scientists are expecting to clone human beings in the near future. However, it is strange that people think that they can recreate human beings but Allah cannot do that on the Day of Judgment and they disbelieve in the Life Hereafter. Islam is unique among other religions in terms of its clear depiction of the Afterlife. In Hinduism, instead of the Life Hereafter, there is a belief in continuous rebirth and punishment in this world in the form of rebirth in inferior forms. Buddhism's concept of Afterlife peaks at "Nirvana" – the supreme state free from suffering and individual existence. It is a state Buddhists refer to as "Enlightenment." The attainment of nirvana breaks the otherwise endless rebirth cycle of reincarnation – a belief not very different from Hinduism's concept of rebirth.

The concepts of paradise and hell are very clear in Islam. Here someone may raise the objection that Italian Christian poet Dante Alighieri (1265 – 1321 CE) wrote The Divine Comedy, a poem which used to be considered a literary masterpiece. In The Divine Comedy, Dante provided a vivid description of the Life Hereafter and paradise and hell. For a long time, people thought of Dante's poem to be an original work

---

[111] Izetbegovic, Alija Ali (1989). *Islam Between East and West.* Indianapolis, American Trust Publications.

although the Life Hereafter is not described to such details in The Holy Bible. However, the dilemma has been resolved now. Professor Miguel Asin, a Catholic Christian priest from Spain, did an in-depth study of the Islamic sources (Qur'an and Prophetic traditions) as well as the works of Spanish Muslim philosophers including Ibn Hazm, Ibn Rusd (Averroes) and the famous Sufi Ibn Arabi. After years of extensive research, he discovered parallels between the Islamic traditions about the Afterlife based on *hadeeth* (traditions of Prophet Muhammad peace be upon him) and The Divine Comedy by the Italian poet Dante Alighieri. The similarities pervade the entire poem and they are far from being superficial. In this book, Prof. Asin concluded that the medieval Italian poet Dante stole the whole description, features and episodes of the Life Hereafter from the *hadeeth* literature relating to Mi'raaj (ascension) of Prophet Muhammad (peace be upon him) to the heavens and the spiritual visions of Ibn Arabi. At the beginning of this discovery about Dante's plagiarism, Prof. Asin (although he is a devoted Christian) faced severe criticism from Roman Catholic clergy, Nationalist Italians and European Christians because this research was showing that their most cherished poem was based on non-Christian sources.[112] However, the proofs presented by Professor Asin in his book are irrefutable and the consensus of opinion of all eminent scholars of Europe and America is now in favor of Prof. Asin's thesis.

This Islamic concept of Afterlife is especially prominent in the surahs (Chapters) of the Qur'an which were revealed in Makkah. This clear depiction of the themes of opposites did not escape the observation of the Japanese non-Muslim researcher of the Qur'an as mentioned in the previous chapter. Professor Toshihiko Izutsu of the Keio University (Tokyo), renowned Japanese philosopher, says in his book *Ethico-Religious Concepts in the Qur'an* that the "theme of opposites" and their comparison are very common in the Qur'an, unlike other religious scriptures. Professor Izutsu states:

---

[112] Asin, Miguel (2001). *Islam and the Divine Comedy.* India, Goodword Books.

*"The Quranic outlook divides all human qualities into two radical-
ly opposed categories.... In fact, throughout the Qur'an there runs the
keynote of dualism regarding the moral values of man: the basic
dualism of believer and unbeliever. In this sense, the ethical system of
Islam is of a very simple structure. For by the ultimate yardstick of
'belief' one can easily decide to which of the two categories a given
person or a given act belongs."*[113]

The "basic dichotomy of moral properties" to which Professor Izutsu
is referring appears in the Quranic verses in a number of different forms.
For instance, that basic dichotomy could be seen between the 'Fellows of
the Right' or 'the Dwellers of Paradise' and 'the Fellows of the Left' or 'the
Dwellers of Hell' as described in the Qur'an:

*"Not equal are the dwellers of the Fire and the dwellers of the
Paradise. It is the dwellers of Paradise that will be successful."* (Surah
Al-Hashr: 20)

Similarly, the Qur'an presents a clear depiction of the dwellers of the
paradise and the inhabitants of the hellfire at various places:

*And those on the Right Hand,
Who will be those on the Right Hand?
(They will be) among thornless lote-trees.
Among Talh (banana-trees) with fruits piled one above another.
In shade long-extended.
By water flowing constantly. And fruit in plenty.
Whose season is not limited, and their supply will not be cut off.
And on couches or thrones, raised high.
Verily, We have created them (maidens) of special creation.
And made them virgins.
Loving (their husbands only),
equal in age.*

---

[113] Izutsu, Toshihiko (2002). *Ethico-Religious Concepts in the Qur'an.* Montreal,
McGill-Queen's University Press.

For those on the Right Hand.
A multitude of those (on the Right Hand)
will be from the first generation (who embraced Islam).
And a multitude of those (on the Right Hand)
will be from the later times (generations).
And those on the Left Hand
Who will be those on the Left Hand?
In fierce hot wind and boiling water.
And shadow of black smoke.
(That shadow) neither cool, nor (even) good.
Verily, before that, they indulged in luxury.
And were persisting in great sin (joining partners in worship along
with Allah, committing murders and other crimes, etc.). And they
used to say: "When we die and become dust and bones, shall we then
indeed be resurrected?"And also our forefathers?"
Say (O Muhammad peace be upon him): "(Yes) verily, those of old,
and those of later times."All will surely be gathered together for
appointed Meeting of a known Day.
(Surah Al-Waaqiah: 27 – 50)

Qur'an even vividly depicts the horrors of the Day of Judgment and standing before the Lord of this universe:

That Day shall you be brought to Judgment,
not a secret of you will be hidden.
Then as for him who will be given his Record in his right hand will
say: "Take, read my Record!
"Surely, I did believe that I shall meet my Account!"
So he shall be in a life, well-pleasing.
In a lofty Paradise.
The fruits in bunches whereof will be low and near at hand.
Eat and drink at ease for that which
you have sent on before you in days past!

But as for him, who will be given his Record in his left hand,
will say: "I wish that I had not been given my Record!
"And that I had never known, how my Account is?
"I wish, would that it had been my end (death)!
"My wealth has not availed me.
"My power and arguments (to defend myself)
have gone from me!"
(It will be said): "Seize him and fetter him.
Then throw him in the blazing Fire.
"Then fasten him with a chain whereof
the length is seventy cubits!"
Verily, He used not to believe in Allah, the Most Great.
And urged not on the feeding of the poor.
So no friend has he here this Day.
Nor any food except filth from the washing of wounds.
(Surah Al-Haaqah: 18 – 36)

The life of this world is a test. Islam teaches its followers to focus on the next life. Islam teaches its followers to learn to delay their gratification in obedience of their Lord and they will be rewarded abundantly in the Life Hereafter. Islam teaches us to be, in a sense, "emotionally intelligent." Islam teaches it followers to learn how to delay their gratifications. The term "emotional intelligence" was popularized by Harvard University psychologist Daniel Goleman in his best-selling book *Emotional Intelligence*.[114] In his book, Goleman quoted the "marshmallow test" conducted by the researchers at Columbia University. In this experiment, four-year-old kids from the Stanford University pre-school were brought to a room and sat in a chair in front of a juicy marshmallow on a table. The experimenter then told them they could eat that one marshmallow now, or get two if they were willing to wait until the experimenter came back from running an errand. The researchers watched those children

---

[114] Goleman, Daniel (1996). *Emotional Intelligence: Why It Can Matter More Than IQ*. New York, Bantam Books.

from the one-way mirror outside. There were kids who tried their best to control themselves from eating the marshmallow. Some of them started talking to their own selves; others started walking in the room. However, there were other kids in the experiment who could not control themselves, went after immediate gratification, grabbed the marshmallow and ate it. The researchers monitored academic progress of those kids for the next 14 years. In this long term "Marshmallow Test", impulse control to delay the desire of immediate gratification turned out to predict how well those kids were doing 14 years later, as they were graduating high school. Those kids who waited and delayed their gratification, compared to those who grabbed the marshmallow, had less trouble delaying gratification and they scored much higher on national exams.[115] The Islamic concept of Afterlife is similar to the above-mentioned situation. Those people who lead their lives according to the commandments set forth by Allah and they know how to delay their gratifications in the situations which involve disobedience of their Lord, they are the ones who are "intelligent" in the Islamic sense. Such are the people about whom Allah says in the Qur'an:

"But for him who fears the standing before his Lord, there will be two *Gardens (i.e., in Paradise)."* (Surah Ar-Rehman: 46)

"But as for him who feared standing before his Lord, and restrained himself from impure evil desires, and lusts. Verily, Paradise will be his abode." (Surah An-Naaziat: 40, 41)

---

[115] Ibid

CHAPTER TEN

The Sun is Rising in the West

I SLAM IS THE FASTEST GROWING RELIGION in the world and has an estimated 1.6 billion followers throughout the world. This includes not only the natural population increase among Muslims but also people of every religion converting to Islam, especially in the Western countries. It seems that the sun is rising in the West. Maryam Jameelah (formerly Margaret Marcos), a Jewish convert to Islam, has made an interesting remark about the phenomenon of conversion to Islam in her well-known book *Quest for the Truth*:

> "Islam is completely different from other religions such as Christianity and Judaism in that whenever the blood of the Muslim nation starts to get cold, it is invigorated by the warmth of the fresh blood of new Muslim converts." [116]

The beauty of Islam lies in the fact that it causes complete transformation in the lives of those who embrace Islam. The people who accept Islam could have been drug addicts, indulged in heavy metal music or living in a prison but as soon as they convert to Islam, a complete change takes place in their lives. We can just look at the Afro-Americans in the U.S.A. as an example. The well-known American writer, James Baldwin, in his best-selling book, *The Fire Next Time*, vividly described the agony of the Black American addict in the following words:

> "I remember my buddies of years ago, in the hallways with their wine and their whiskey and their tears, in hallways still frozen on the needle, and my brother saying to me once, if Harlem didn't have so many churches and junkies, there would be blood flowing in streets." [117]

---

[116] Jameelah, Maryam (1989). *Quest for the Truth: Memoirs of Childhood and Youth in America*. Lahore, Mohammad Yusuf Khan & Sons.
[117] Baldwin, James (1962). *The Fire Next Time*. London, Penguin Books.

143

However, after such drug addicts convert to Islam and absorb the spiritual message of Islam, their lives immediately change in ways which all the governmental educational, psychological and welfare institutions fail to achieve. James Baldwin notes that Islam

"has been able to do what generations of welfare workers and committees and resolutions and reports and housing projects and playgrounds have failed to do: to heal and redeem drunkards and junkies, to convert people who have come out of prisons and keep them out, to make men chaste and women virtuous, and to invest both male and female with the pride and serenity that hang about them like unfailing light." [118]

This chapter is devoted to the stories of some of the well-known converts to Islam in the recent times. These converts to Islam have found happiness and peace of mind in Islam. They have found the answers to the questions of life in Islam. When they studied Islam, they found out that Islam is in fact the religion of truth which is from God Almighty and the best way of life.

MOHAMMAD ASAD (LEOPOLD WEISS)

Mohammad Asad (1900-92) was an Austrian Jew, named Leopold Weiss at birth. He accepted Islam in the year 1926. Muhammad Asad was no ordinary convert. He tried to affect the course of contemporary Islam, as an author, activist, diplomat, and translator of the Qur'an. Muhammad Asad died in February 1992 at the age of ninety-one, so that his career may be said to have paralleled the emergence of every trend in contemporary Islam.

Muhammad Asad was born Leopold Weiss in July 1900 in the city of Lvov (German Lemberg), now in Poland, then part of the Austrian Empire. He was the descendant of a long line of rabbis. Asad himself received a thorough religious education so that he would carry on the family's rabbinical tradition. He became proficient in Hebrew at an early

---

[118] Ibid.

age. He had studied the Old Testament in the original as well as the text and commentaries of the Talmud, the Mishna and Gemara. After living in Vienna for a while, he left Europe for the Middle East in 1922 for what was supposed to be a short visit to an uncle in Jerusalem. There he came to know and like the Arabs and was struck by how Islam infused their everyday lives with profound meaning, spiritual strength and inner peace.

At the young age of 22, Weiss became a correspondent for the *Frankfurter Zeitung,* one of the most prestigious newspapers of Germany and Europe. As a journalist, he traveled extensively to the Middle Eastern countries. Weiss's interest in Islam increased not only because of his first hand knowledge by meeting the Muslim people and his curiosity but also because he felt, in his words, "a spiritual emptiness, a vague, cynical relativism born out of increasing hopelessness" from which he needed to escape.

Back in Berlin from the Middle East a few years later, Weiss underwent a spiritual experience, which he wrote some 30 years later:

"One day—it was in September 1926—Elsa [Asad's wife] and I found ourselves traveling in the Berlin subway. It was an upper-class compartment. My eye fell casually on a well-dressed man opposite me, apparently a well-to-do-businessman.... I thought idly how well the portly figure of this man fitted into the picture of prosperity which one encountered everywhere in Central Europe in those days: ...Most of the people were now well dressed and well fed, and the man opposite me was therefore no exception. But when I looked at his face, I did not seem to be looking at a happy face. He appeared to be worried: and not merely worried but acutely unhappy, with eyes staring vacantly ahead and the corners of his mouth drawn in as if in pain—but not in bodily pain. Not wanting to be rude, I turned my eyes away and saw next to him a lady of some elegance. She also had a strangely unhappy expression on her face, as if contemplating or experiencing something that caused her pain.... And then I began to look around at all other faces in the compartment—faces belonging without exception to well-dressed, well-fed people: and in almost every one of them I could discern an expression of hidden suffering, so hidden that the owner of the face seemed to be quite unaware of it....The impression was so strong that I mentioned it to Elsa; and she too began to look around with the careful eyes of a painter accustomed to study human features. Then she turned to me, astonished, and said: 'You are right.... I wonder, do they know themselves what is going on in them?'...

I knew that they did not—for otherwise they could not go on wasting their lives as they did, without any faith in binding truths, without any goal beyond the desire to raise their own 'standard of living,' without any hopes other than having more material amenities, more gadgets, and perhaps more power....

When we returned home, I happened to glance at my desk on which lay open a copy of the Koran I had been reading earlier. Mechanically, I picked the book up to put it away, but just as I was about to close it, my eyes fell on the open page before me, and I read:

You are obsessed by greed for more and more
Until you go down to your graves.
Nay, but you will come to know!
And once again: Nay, but you will come to know!
Nay, if you but knew it with the knowledge of certainty,
You would indeed see the hell you are in.
In time, indeed, you shall see it with the eye of certainty:
And on that Day you will be asked what you have done with the boon of life.

For a moment I was speechless. I think that the book shook in my hands. Then I handed it to Elsa. 'Read this. Is it not an answer to what we saw in the subway?' "It was an answer so decisive that all doubt was suddenly at an end. I knew now, beyond any doubt, that it was a God-inspired book I was holding in my hand: for although it had been placed before man over thirteen centuries ago, it clearly anticipated something that could have become true only in this complicated, mechanized, phantom-ridden age of ours.

At all times people had known greed: but at no time before had greed outgrown a mere eagerness to acquire things and become an obsession that blurred the sight of everything else: an irresistible craving to get, to do, to contrive more and more—more today than yesterday, and more tomorrow than today: ...and that hunger, that insatiable hunger for ever new goals gnawing at man's soul: Nay, if you but knew it you would see the hell you are in....

This, I saw, was not the mere human wisdom of a man of a distant past in distant Arabia. However wise he may have been, such a man could not by himself have foreseen the torment so peculiar to this twentieth century. Out of the Koran spoke a voice greater than the voice of Muhammad...." [119]

Thus, Weiss became a Muslim. He converted in Berlin and took the names Muhammad, to honor the Prophet, and Asad—meaning "lion"— as a reminder of his given name. After accepting Islam, Asad and his wife, Elsa, who also converted, set off on pilgrimage to Makkah.

Asad spent some six years in the holy cities of Makkah and Madinah, where he studied Arabic, the Qur'an, *hadeeth* (the traditions of the Prophet) and Islamic history. Those studies led him to "the firm conviction that Islam, as a spiritual and social phenomenon, is still, in spite of all the drawbacks caused by the deficiencies of the Muslims, by far the greatest driving force mankind has ever experienced." [120]

---

[119] Asad, Muhammad (2002). *The Road to Mecca*. Malaysia, Islamic Book Trust.
[120] Ibid.

His academic knowledge of classical Arabic – made easier by familiarity with Hebrew and Aramaic – was further enhanced by his wide travels and his contacts in Arabia with Bedouins. To study Muslim communities and cultures further east, Asad left Arabia for India in 1932. There he met the celebrated poet-philosopher Muhammad Iqbal, the spiritual progenitor of Pakistan. Iqbal persuaded Asad to stay on "to help elucidate the intellectual premises of the future Islamic state...." [121] Asad stayed in India and, after 1947, in Pakistan for a few more years until he moved to New York.

Among Asad's notable written works are, The Road to Mecca (his autobiography), Islam at the Crossroads and translation and exegesis, or tafseer, of the Qur'an in English (a culmination of his 17 years of tireless research). He continued to serve Islam till his death in Spain on February 23, 1992.

MARYAM JAMEELAH (MARGARET MARCOS)

Maryam Jameelah was born Margaret Marcus to a Jewish family in New Rochelle, New York, on May 23, 1934. She grew up in a secular environment, but at the age of nineteen, while a student at New York University, she developed a keen interest in religion. Unable to find spiritual guidance in her immediate environment, she looked to other faiths. Her search brought her into contact with a wide range of religious cults and world religions. She became acquainted with Islam around 1954. She was greatly impressed by Marmaduke Pickthall's The Meaning of the Glorious Koran and by the works of Muhammad Asad, himself a convert from Judaism to Islam. Jameelah regarded Mohammad Asad's The Road to Mecca and Islam at Crossroads as profound influences on her decision to become a Muslim.

She embraced Islam in New York in 1961, and soon after started to write for the Muslim Digest of Durban, South Africa. Her articles outlined a pristine and pure view of Islam. Through the journal, Jameelah became acquainted with the works of Syed Abu Ala Maudoodi, Islamic scholar from Pakistan. Jameelah traveled to Pakistan in 1962 on Syed Maudoodi's advice. Since settling in Pakistan, she has written various books

---

[121] Asad, Muhammad (2002). *The Road to Mecca.* Malaysia, Islamic Book Trust.

on Islamic ideology. Today she lives in Lahore and continues to write on Islamic thought and life.

YUSUF ISLAM (FORMER POP SINGER CAT STEVENS)

Cat Stevens (born on July 21, 1948, and now named Yusuf Islam) is best known for his tenure as a popular British singer. He grew up in London. At the outset of his musical career, Steven Demetre Georgiou adopted the Cat Stevens moniker. During his studies at Art College, he was tested by a record producer, Mike Hurst, formerly of the pop-folk trio of the Springfields. Mike was impressed by the performance of the young artist, which marked the beginning of Cat Stevens' musical career. As Cat Stevens, he sold forty million albums, mostly in the 1960s and 1970s. His most notable songs include "Morning Has Broken", "Peace Train", "Moon shadow", "Wild World", "Father and Son", "Matthew and Son", "The First Cut is the Deepest", and "Oh Very Young."

Following a bout of TB early in his career, he undertook an ongoing search for peace and ultimate spiritual truth about which he writes in his autobiography:

"It wasn't long before I had my first couple of hit records; my name and photo was splashed all over the media, and I was on the road. But that very short and speedy period of exposure to success had its pitfalls. Although I was basically an introvert and extremely shy, my publicists were busy at work, making me larger than real life. The public then expected me to live up to this image, so the only way was for me to resort to intoxicants. I lost control. Staying up late, drinking, partying, and smoking endless cigarettes – I fell sick and contracted Tuberculosis. Within a year I found myself in hospital lying on my back. The pop business was whizzing past me and I was left there to think: 'What happened?' I became aware of my own mortality and the inevitability of death." [122]

[122] Islam, Yusuf (1995-99). *My journey from Cat Stevens to Yusuf Islam: The Background Story*. London, Mountain of Light.

However, after a year of recovery, he went back into the music and singing business. Then, an incident happened in his life that proved to be a major turning point in his life. Cat Stevens was swimming in the Pacific Ocean at Malibu (Los Angeles area). He did not realize that it was the wrong time to swim. All of a sudden he found out that the currents of water were moving him away from the shore. He felt his body was helpless. In his own words:

"My body was absolutely powerless. I saw my manager standing there thinking everything was all right, but I could not communicate to him. Finally, in a split second, I realized I had no other help and I shouted out, "O God, if you save me, I'll work for you!" and at that moment, a wave came from behind me and pushed me forward. Suddenly, with all the energy that I needed, I was swimming back to land and within a few minutes, I was there: safe and alive. That was a moment of truth. I knew that God existed and, in a way, I renewed my relationship with Him at that moment." [123]

His chance to fulfill that promise came when he received a translation of the Qur'an as a gift from his elder brother, David. His spiritual quest for answers was fulfilled and he embraced Islam in December, 1977. Six months later he changed his name to Yusuf Islam, walked away from the media career to start a new life and raise a family.

Today, Yusuf Islam is undoubtedly one of the world's most famous converts to Islam. He has done pioneering work to support Islamic education throughout Great Britain. The three schools he founded in London's Brent district – Islamia Primary, Islamia Girls' Secondary and the Brondesbury College for Boys – are ranked consistently as the top in the borough's examination league tables. In addition, his U.N.-registered charity, Small Kindness, provides humanitarian relief efforts, by providing direct aid as well as supporting social and educational programs, to orphans and families in Bosnia, Kosovo, Iraq and other countries of the

[123] Ibid.

world. In addition, he lectures extensively through out the world to spread the light of Islam. Commenting on his life transforming experience, Yusuf Islam once noted:

"I tried Zen and Ching, numerology, tarot cards and astrology. I tried to look back into the Bible and could not find anything. When I received the Qur'an, a guidance that would explain everything to me - who I was; what was the purpose of life; what was the reality and what would be the reality; and where I came from - I realized that this was the true religion; religion not in the sense the West understands it, not the type for only your old age. In the West, whoever wishes to embrace a religion and make it his only way of life is deemed a fanatic. I was not a fanatic; I was at first confused between the body and the soul. Then I realized that the body and soul are not apart and you don't have to go to the mountain to be religious. We must follow the will of God. Then we can rise higher than the angels. The first thing I wanted to do now was to be a Muslim."[124]

MALCOLM X (EL-HAJJ MALIK EL-SHABBAZ)

Malcolm was a civil rights activist and religious leader. In 1964, after a pilgrimage to Mecca, he announced his conversion to orthodox Islam and his belief in the possibility of brotherhood between blacks and whites. Upon returning to America, Malcolm X embarked on a mission to enlighten both blacks and whites with his new views. Malcolm X recognized that in order to truly learn from the *Hajj*, its inherent spiritual lessons must be extended not only to Muslims but also to non-Muslims.

"...America needs to understand Islam, because this is the one religion that erases from its society the race problem. Throughout my travels in the Muslim world, I have met, talked to, and even eaten with people who in America would have been considered white -- but the "white" attitude was removed from their minds by

---

[124] www.catstevens.com

the religion of Islam. I have never before seen sincere and true brotherhood practiced by all colors together, irrespective of their color. My pilgrimage broadened my scope. It blessed me with a new insight. In two weeks in the Holy Land, I saw what I never had seen in thirty-nine years here in America. I saw all races, all colors, – blue-eyed blonds to black-skinned Africans – in true brotherhood! In unity! Living as one! Worshipping as one! No segregationists."[125]

DR. GARY MILLER (ABDUL-AHAD OMAR)

Dr Gary Miller (Abdul-Ahad Omar) is a Canadian Muslim. He is notable for being a former Christian theologian, mathematician and minister who converted to Islam. He was active in Christian missionary work at a particular point of his life but he soon began to discover many inconsistencies in the Bible. In 1978, he happened to read the Qur'an expecting that it, too, would contain a mixture of truth and falsehood.

He discovered to his amazement that the message of the Qur'an was precisely the same as the essence of truth that he had distilled from the Bible. He became a Muslim and since then has been active in giving public presentations on Islam including radio and television appearances. He is also the author of several articles and publications about Islam.

SHEIKH YUSUF ESTES

Renowned Islamic scholar, Sheikh Yusuf Estes, was born into a very strong Christian family in the Midwest region (U.S.A.). His family and his ancestors not only built the churches and schools across the U.S.A. but also they actually were the same ones who came here in the first place. While he was still in elementary school, they relocated to Houston, Texas in 1949. During his youth, he became very interested in different types of music, especially Gospel and Classical music. Because his whole family was religious and musical, it followed that he too would begin his studies in both areas. All this set him for the logical position of Music Minister in many of the churches that he became affiliated with over the years.

---

[125] X, Malcolm (1992). *The Autobiography of Malcolm X.* New York, Ballantine Books.

Being a great musician due to his education and experience, Sheikh Yusuf Estes started teaching keyboard musical instruments in 1960. By the year 1963, he owned his own studios in Laurel, Maryland, called "Estes Music Studios." The other businesses Sheikh Estes and his father owned included Estes Music Company and Estes Piano & Organ Co. He and his father used to established music stores, TV and radio programs and outdoor entertainments for fun and profit. Their primary target was to sell musical instruments across the country. He was also a member of NAAMM (National Association of American Music Manufactures).[126]

In 1991, Sheikh Estes had the opportunity to have an Arab Muslim businessman named Mohammad, as a paying guest. Sheikh Estes had many doubts about Islam spread by the media. Mohammad clarified all his doubts. Eventually, Sheikh Estes embraced Islam along with his wife and children as well as his parents. After becoming a Muslim, he studied the Islamic sciences very diligently. Presently, he is the National Muslim Chaplain for American Muslims, sponsored by a number of organizations in Washington, DC, especially concentrating his efforts in the institutional areas such as military, universities and prisons. In addition, he travels around the entire world lecturing and sharing the message of Islam.

HAMZA YUSUF HANSON

Hamza Yusuf Hanson was born in Washington State and raised in Northern California. He was baptized Greek Orthodox by his parents. Both his parents are highly educated. He himself went to a Jesuit school at Georgetown Preparatory School. During his teenage years, he got in a serious car accident after which he started to learn about the Afterlife. At one stage, he even attended Christian missionary researcher Dr. Raymond Moody's lectures about the near death experiences. However, nothing satisfied him. He had not learned about Islam until then. Then, an interesting thing happened as it was narrated by Hamza Yusuf Hanson in Steven Barboza's book *American Jihad: Islam After Malcolm X*. Sheikh

---

[126] Estes, Yusuf (2006). *Personal Email Communication.* Washington D.C.

Hamza Yusuf was looking for some books in a used-book store when his eyes caught sight of a little Qur'an's translation sitting on the bottom shelf. He said to himself that that is the only religion about which he did not know anything. Therefore, he purchased the Qur'an and read in its introduction that Muslims believe in a very simple creed: "There is no god except One God and Muhammad is His messenger." Then, Hamza Yusuf looked in the Table of Contents and saw the chapter of Mary. He was surprised to know that Muslims in fact believed in Mary. He also saw the names of other Biblical prophets in the Qur'an which he already knew. Then, he started reading the "chapter of Mary" from the Qur'an and when he reached the Qur'anic verse where God says: "The likeness of Jesus is the likeness of Adam. That God only says to a thing: Be, and it is.", Hamza Yusuf had a realization about which he said: "It was kind of negating the Son of God thing that I'd always had a hard time with. And all the Christians that I'd met that have converted to Islam – they'd always said that." [127]

Sheikh Hamza Yusuf accepted Islam a week after that incident and it was the year 1977. Soon thereafter he traveled to the Muslim world and studied for ten years in the U. A. E., Saudi Arabia, as well as North and West Africa. He received teaching licenses in various Islamic subjects from several well-known scholars in various countries. After ten years of studies abroad, he returned to the USA and took degrees in Religious Studies and Health Care. He is the founder of Zaytuna Institute (California) which is dedicated to the revival of traditional study methods and the sciences of Islam. In an interview with Steven Barboza, Sheikh Hamza Yusuf explained the importance of education in Islam:

> "Islam has never had that fear of educating people. It wasn't built on a structure of exploitation. It was built on a structure of liberation – liberation through education, through critical understanding." [128]

[127] Barboza, Steven (1993). *American Jihad: Islam After Malcolm X.* New York, Doubleday Dell Publishing Group.
[129] Ibid.

Sheikh Hamza Yusuf has studied various Islamic sciences from the classical Muslim scholars across the world. He has translated into modern English several classical Arabic traditional texts and poems. Sheikh Hamza Hanson explained to the American author Steven Barboza how Islam gave the rights to the oppressed segments of the society 1400 years ago which are being recognized by the world only now:

> "The injunctions that were put into the Qur'an were radical at that time – like giving women the right to inherit. That was a very radical departure from the norm. Women didn't get the right to inherit in Western civilization until the 19th century.
>
> There's a story that the people of Mecca said to one of the companions of the Prophet, 'We heard that he's giving your women rights. Next he's going to be giving your animals rights.' This companion retorted, 'He has. We can't give them a burden more than they can bear on their backs.'
>
> The Prophet [Muhammad peace be upon him] is described in the Qur'an as the mercy for all the worlds, which includes the animal kingdom and the vegetable kingdom." [129]

[129] Barboza, Steven (1993). *American Jihad: Islam After Malcolm X*. New York, Doubleday Dell Publishing Group.

CHAPTER ELEVEN

Prophet Muhammad's (peace be upon him) Last Sermon

THIS BOOK IS CONCLUDED WITH the farewell sermon which Prophet Muhammad (peace be upon him) delivered on the occasion of his last pilgrimage to the Holy City of Makkah in the year 632 CE. There were more than 100,000 men and women attending that gathering. This sermon was delivered on the Ninth day of Dhul al Hijjah 10 A.H. in the valley of Mount Arafat in Makkah:

After praising and thanking God, Prophet Muhammad (peace be upon him) said:

"O People, listen well to my words, for I do not know whether, after this year, I shall ever be amongst you again. Therefore listen to what I am saying to you very carefully and TAKE THESE WORDS TO THOSE WHO COULD NOT BE PRESENT HERE TODAY.

O People, just as you regard this month, this day, this city as Sacred, so regard the life and property of every Muslim as a sacred trust. Return the goods entrusted to you to their rightful owners. Treat others justly so that no one would be unjust to you. Remember that you will indeed meet your LORD, and that HE will indeed reckon your deeds. God has forbidden you to take usury (riba), therefore all riba obligations shall henceforth be waived. Your capital, however, is yours to keep. You will neither inflict nor suffer inequity. God has judged that there shall be no riba and that all the riba due to `Abbas ibn `Abd al Muttalib shall henceforth be waived.

Every right arising out of homicide in pre-Islamic days is henceforth waived and the first such right that I waive is that arising from the murder of Rabi`ah ibn al Harith ibn `Abd al Muttalib.

O Men, the Unbelievers indulge in tampering with the calendar in order to make permissible that which God forbade, and to forbid that which God has made permissible. With God the months are twelve in number. Four of them are sacred, three of these are successive and one occurs singly between the months of Jumada and Sha`ban. Beware of the devil, for the safety of your religion. He has lost all hope that he will ever be able to lead you astray in big things, so beware of following him in small things.

O People, it is true that you have certain rights over your women, but they also have rights over you. Remember that you have taken them as your wives only under God's trust and with His permission. If they abide by your right then to them belongs the right to be fed and clothed in kindness. Treat your women well and be kind to them, for they are your partners and committed helpers. It is your right and they do not make friends with anyone of whom you do not approve, as well as never to be unchaste...

O People, listen to me in earnest, worship God (The One Creator of the Universe), perform your five daily prayers (*Salah*), fast during the month of Ramadan, and give your financial obligation (*Zakah*) of your wealth. Perform *Hajj* if you can afford to.

All mankind is from Adam and Eve, an Arab has no superiority over a non-Arab nor a non-Arab has any superiority over an Arab; also a white has no superiority over a black nor a black has any superiority over white except by piety and good action.

Learn that every Muslim is a brother to every Muslim and that

Muslims constitute one brotherhood. Nothing shall be legitimate to a Muslim which belongs to a fellow Muslim unless it was given freely and willingly. Do not, therefore, do injustice to yourselves.

Remember, one day you will appear before God (The Creator) and you will answer for your deeds. So beware, do not stray from the path of righteousness after I am gone.

O People, NO PROPHET OR MESSENGER WILL COME AFTER ME AND NO NEW FAITH WILL BE BORN. Reason well, therefore, O People, and understand words which I convey to you. I am leaving you with the Book of God (the QUR'AN) and my SUNNAH (the life style and the behavioral mode of the Prophet), if you follow them you will never go astray.

All those who listen to me shall pass on my words to others and those to others again; and may the last ones understand my words better than those who listen to me directly. Be my witness O God, that I have conveyed your message to your people.

APPENDIX

Glossary of Islamic Terms

ALLAH The Arabic word "Allah" is equivalent to "God" in English. However, linguistically, the word "Allah" is much more precise than "God" in its meanings. There is no gender, male or female, associated with the word "Allah" in Arabic whereas the term "God" is masculine and its feminine is "goddess." Similarly, there is no plural for "Allah" whereas the plural for "God" is "gods." The word "Allah" is a proper and the true Name of God, through which man calls upon God personally. The name "Allah" is not confined to Islam; it is also the Name by which Arabic-speaking Christians of the Oriental churches call upon God.

FIQH Islamic jurisprudence

IMAM (also Sheikh) Title given to an Islamic scholar

IMAAN Faith.

HADEETH (plural: Ahadeeth) The collection of recorded saying and actions of the Prophet Muhammad (peace be upon him). Famous books of *hadeeth* include Bukhari, Muslim, Abu Dawud, Nisai, Ibn Majah, Musnad Ahmed, Tirmidhi, Ibn Habban

HALAL That which is lawful, particularly income, personal activities, food and meat from animals that have been ritually slaughtered. The opposite is haram.

HARAM That which is prohibited

QUR'AN The last and Final Book that Allah revealed for mankind. It was revealed over a period of twenty-three years to Prophet Muhammad (peace be upon him).

SAHIH Authentic, sound. In *hadeeth* terminology, it refers to authentic reports/traditions of Prophet Muhammad (peace be upon him).

SALAH The prescribed act of worship in Islam, which includes the acts of standing, bowing and prostrating before God.

SAWM The word "*saw'm*" means to abstain from something. In the Islamic commandments, "*saw'm*" or fasting means to abstain from drinking, eating and sexual relations with one's spouse from before sunrise until sunset.

SHARIAH Revealed law. The canonical law of Islam as put forth in the Qur'an and the sunnah and elaborated by Islamic scholars

SUNNAH It refers to the spoken and acted example of the Prophet Muhammad (peace be upon him). It includes what he approved, allowed, or condoned and what he himself refrained from and disapproved of.

SURAH It refers to the chapters of the Holy Qur'an. There are a total of 114 surahs in the Qur'an, some of them are short while others are long.

TAFSEER Commentary on the Holy Qur'an

TAWHEED The doctrine of the "Oneness of God." This is a central tenet of Islam, upon which all other beliefs and doctrines are based.

ZAKAH *Zakah* literally means "purification" and "growth." In the Islamic teachings, zakah or alms-giving is the practice of charitable giving by Muslims based on accumulated wealth. Zakah consists of spending a fixed portion of one's wealth for the benefit of the poor or needy.